HEMU AND HIS TIMES
(Afghans vs Mughals)

HEMU AND HIS TIMES
(Afghans vs Mughals)

M.L. Bhargava

RELIANCE PUBLISHING HOUSE
NEW DELHI

ISBN : 81-85047-93-6

Published By :
Lion Dr. S.K. Bhatia
for **RELIANCE PUBLISHING HOUSE**
3026/7H, Ranjit Nagar,
New Delhi-110008 Ph. 5722605

Composed By :
SURI TYPESETTERS
2-A, Kanchenjunga Building,
18 Bara Khamba Road, New Delhi-1. Ph. 2217096

Printed By :
EFFICIENT OFFSET PRINTERS
New Delhi

Contents

CHAPTERS

Foreword

There are certain glorious periods in the long annals of India which remain either fully or partially unexplored. Such is the period that falls between the reigns of Sher Shah Suri and Akbar who occupy a special position in the history of India. Consequently, the role of the Afghans vis-a-vis the Mughals, as the author of the book Dr. M.L. Bhargava observes, remains obscure in the tangled web of the times. It is also significant that this approach almost obliterates the significant place of Hemu, who finds a mention only in passing or as a footnote while narrating the achievements of Akbar. It is this lacuna in historical scholarship that the learned author tries to fill through the present work. His learned exposition as to why and how this has occurred and has persisted for so long makes fascinating reading. It is by itself a contribution to historiography. He gives due credit to Dr. K.R. Kanungo and Dr. Nirod Bhushan Roy for their pioneering attempts to illumine these dark corners to some extent. The aforesaid research work was however, done in the thirties by these scholars.

The comprehensive role of Hemu, who fought and won twentytwo battles and assumed the legendary title of Raja Vikramajeet, remains still to be highlighted as an honest tribute to history. The inspiration to do research in this area came to the author in 1959 from the late Dr. K.M. Munshi, the scholar, lawyer and statesman who was at that time the Governor of U.P. As the author mentions, this prompted him to write first a biography of Hemu in Hindi in 1961 and later on in English. Both these books were widely acclaimed as a fresh contribution to the study of Indian history. But they had been unavailable for long and the research and interest of Dr. Bhargava in the subject continued. Some new material has been unearthed. The learned author discusses at some length about the different and variegated source material that he has used in this historical reconstruction in the present work. This speaks adequately about his wide reading and painstaking effort. He has not only utilised the earlier material but also sundry academic researches related to the subject and carried out recently in the academic world. Hence, the present work, though a revised edition technically, is almost new in its comprehensiveness of approach and presentation.

The name of Hemu does inspire a sense of pride not because of any myths but because of his personality, valour and vision. He was like a brilliant meteor, which flashed on the historical sky of the country. The sectarian historical prejudices must give way before the torch of truth. In painting the colourful period, Dr. Bhargava, in the wide perspective of his coverage, provides a lively vividness and veracity to the happenings and the concerned personalities. While tracing the lineaments of the birth and parentage, rise to power and glory of Hemu as well as of his accomplishments, the author also tries to bring out the conflicting roles of the Afghans and the Moghuls of the period in its proper perspective. The chapters on the fateful Second Battle of Panipat and Hemu's martyrdom are replete with information of historic authenticity and are moving at human level as well as in historical context. The book does not end with Hemu's tragic death but critically analyses subsequent developments of significance to medieval Indian history. The attempt of Akbar at reconciliation with Hemu's descendants through a Firman, issued in 1563 A.D., is included in the book is notable. The detailed bibliography and the appendices add to the value of this well-researched work.

Dr. M.L. Bhargava, a distinguished historian, and biographer has a number of works to his credit. In the present work, he carries further the tradition of objective research and scholarship. The learned author deserves our appreciation for his new volume on "Hemu And His Times" and, I do hope that it will be greatly welcome not only by historians and scholars but also by readers in general who value heroism and chivalry in human affairs and have a sense of legitimate pride in the history of our nation.

18th January, 1991.

T.N. Chaturvedi
New Delhi,

Introduction

The period covered by Hemu, on account of its falling between two illustrious reigns of Sher Shah and Akbar, has not received the attention it deserved. It has also been wrongly held that after Sher Shah the Afghan empire broke up, although his son Islam Shah ruled for eight years, his period had not been studied in depth. Again, after the death of Islam Shah, when his kingdom was tossed to and from between as many as three contenders, and Adil Shah had abrogated all his authority, civil and military to Hemu, the material has not been pieced together.

Consequently an erroneous impression has been created by historians that the Mughal dynasty once founded in 1526 continued right through, with only a brief Sur interregnum. It was conveniently overlooked that this period from 1540 to 1555-56 was more than the rule of the first two Mughals i.e. from 1526 to 1540. Naturally the part played by the Afghans vis a vis the Mughals was obscured by tangled history. The select extracts translated by Elliot and Dowson only laid emphasis on foul murders, campaigns and sieges. And Hemu's performances during the last few years of Islam Shah and during Adil Shah's nominal suzerainty, were obliterated by Mughal historians' prejudicial accounts about his heredity and low origin. That this calumny had continued for over four hundred years is astounding as well as unfortunate.

The earliest to break the sod were Dr. K.R. Qanungo and Nirod Bhushan Roy. Whilst the former highlighted the achievements of Sher Shah, the later worked hard to pen down the history of the successors of Sher Shah, viz Islam Shah, Adil Shah and Hemu. It was Roy who brought to light Islam Shah's liberal policy towards Hindus, the further development of the excellent administrative system founded by Sher Shah, the ascendancy of Hemu and his lieutenants like Ramaya, Mahipal and Bhagwan Das. The excellent work done by Todarmal Khatri of Lahore in building the fort of Rohtas in hostile Gakkar territory under Sher Shah and Islam Shah was little known. Nirod Bhushan Roy published his work in 1934. Dr. Qanungo first wrote his work on Sher Shah and then brought his excellent book entitled *Sher Shah and His Times.*

As a result of casual work on the successors of Sher Shah, Hemu's achievements had been ignored. It was in 1960-61 that the first biographies in Hindi and English entitled Hemu and His Times were brought out by the author. An attempt was made to piece together the matter lying in obscure details. That Hemu was a conqueror of twenty-two battles was not given the importance that it deserved. That he was the only Hindu king who assumed the title of Raja Vikramajeet was never applauded. Hemu's geneology and his high descent was also not unearthed. The reconciliation attempted by Akbar with Hemu's discendents, by issue of a *Firman* in 1563 A.D. was skipped over by historians. No body ever attempted to contact his descendents at Rewari and near about places for geneological details.

Nirod Bhushan Roy and Dr. Qanungo were the earliest to unravel the details about Hemu's career. But it was only in 1959 that Dr. K.M. Munshi, Rajyapal, Uttar Pradesh expressed a desire that someone might work on Hemu, and the present author wrote a biography first in Hindi and thereafter in English in 1961. In this first attempt effort was made to collect together all available relevant material concerning Hemu's biography from all possible sources. The main objective was to present a connected coherant, picture of the great warrior, a general who knew no defeat, and a successful statesmen of the sixteenth century, so that the students and general readers might evaluate his achievements and wash off the calumny surrounding his name.

The soure-material which was utilised in the first editions and now after a lapse of thirty years in the second revised edition, have been drawn from the following sources :-

1. Persian manuscripts, original as well as in English and Hindi translations, of the contemporary Mughal chroniclers, writers and the servants of the State.
2. Persian manuscripts of various histories written of Afghans, and by Afghan chroniclers, mostly in English translations.
3. Memoirs of Rulers, like Babur, Jehangir and their family members, e.g. Gul-Badan as well as servants of the State, like Jauhar.
4. The Hindi sources of poets and narrators of the Bhakti movement, as well as courtier historians.
5. The Geneological Tables supplied by Hemu's descendents and recent publications like Souvenir's by the community, particularly on the centenary of their Sabha (Association).
6. Local sources like the Annals and Antiquities of Rajasthan as the Central and Western Rajput States of India as well as the Monuments and antiquities of North Western Provinces of Agra and Oudh by the Archaeological Survey of India.

A detailed description of the sources is attempted in the following pages :-

Mughal Sources : As no official history of the Sur dynasty and the successors of Sher Shah, was written under the patronage of the Sur kings or the redoubtable Afghans nobles, their history can be culled only from the chronicles left by the Mughal historians of the age of Akbar. This is as much true about Hemu as of his patrons Islam Shah and Adil Shah. Most of the details about Hemu are available only in Abul Fazl's works, *Akbar-nama* and *Ain-i-Akbari.* As he had all the facilities of a courtier historian he could secure, reliable information about Hemu from the local officials. Although it is not known as to when he started the work of collecting material, but he had completed his monumental work in 1596 A.D. (1004 A.H.), i.e. a few years before Akbar's death and forty years after Hemu's death.

Abul Fazl obtained material from "the old members of the illustrious family and the servants of the State". According to him, he "examined both prudent truth speaking old men and active-minded, right actioned young ones and reduce their statements to writing. The royal command was issued to the provinces (Subahs) that those who from old service remembered with certainty or with admixture of doubts, the events of the past, should copy out their notes and memoranda and submit them to Court." There is no doubt that Abul Fazl's works rank very high both in originality of presentation and marshalling of facts of historical value despite his rhetoric and adulation of his hero.

Abul Fazl believed in Akbar as saints believed in God, hence his narrative is subjective. His primary aim was to exalt the boy emperor and embellish him with divinity of the highest order. As at the time of Hemu's execution, after the second battle of Panipat, Akbar was only 13 years of age, Abul Fazl has given meticulous details of his adversary in order to glorify his hero, although Akbar did not fight any of the battles against him.

While recounting the events leading to the battle of Panipat in 1556 A.D., Abul Fazl has meticulously and assiduously collected all available details about Hemu's army, before and after the battle of Delhi won by him on October 6th 1556. But for the praise lavished by Abul Fazl, history would not have known that Hemu was a conqueror of twenty-two battles for his master Adil Shah. Battle of Delhi was fought by Hemu independently and he proclaimed himself as king of Delhi – thereafter.

Details have been given about his preparations to meet the challenge of the advancing Mughal hordes from Punjab. In view of the Mughal's defeat at Delhi, flight and subsequent execution of Tardi Beg Khan, Abul Fazl has not given details of twenty-nine days of Hemu's rule at Delhi. However in order to highlight the achievements of his hero after the battle of Panipat fought on 5th November 1556, Abul Fazl has again given copious details of Hemu's army, its disposition and even the names of generals and elephants involved. Amongst the Mughal sources, Abul Fazl's works are the primary source about Hemu, his achievements, his father and his birth place etc. Abul Fazl has not hesitated to state that Hemu assumed the airs of royalty, usurped power from the Afghan Sultan Adil Shah and proclaimed himself Raja Vikramaditya. He has only hesitated to say that Hemu set himself as an independent king and struck coins. However he had recognized that "On none of these occasions was there *a ruler of India* possessed of such courage, enterprise and plan..."

Other contemporary Sources : Al-Badaoni's equally comprehensive work entitled, *Muntakhabu-T-Tawarikh* is another source from which details are available about Hemu and His Times. As there is a remarkable corroboration of Abul Fazl's narrative by Al-Badaoni, in respect of Hemu's ups and downs, the authenticity of the account has been well established. The latest attempt by the renowned Sanskrit Scholar Rahul Sankratayan to challenge their details about Hemu's birth place, parentage etc. is simply ridiculous. The theory of Hemu belonging to Rauniyar Vansa of Behar is not even worth examining. It is based on a figment of imagination and the great warrior Hemu remains essentially the one, about whom we have details from Abul Fazl, corroborated by Al-Badaoni.

Al-Badaoni born in 1540 A.D. at Badaun, died in 1615 A.D. He has left a fuller account of this period than any other historian. But his narrative could only see the light of the day after Akbar's death. As a boy he was an eyewitness to Islam Shah's durbars, where the shoes of Islam Shah were saluted and his regulations proclaimed.

Besides Abul Fazl and Al-Badaoni's monumental works, Nizam Uddin's *Tabakat-i-Akbari* or *Akbar Shahi,* also known as *Tarikh-i-Nizami* has also given details about Akbar's reign and valuable comments about Hemu and his relations with the Afghans and the Sur kings. His work was completed in 1593-94 A.D. He has given a very meagre account of the Surs -----a bare narrative of events.

Memoirs of the Mughal emperors, their family members and their servants, are equally important, so far as information is concerned about Hemu's exploits and achievements. Even Babur's memoirs, *Tuzuk-i-Babari,* which gives copious details about the northern India, its flora and fauna, has given information about the region of Mewat, from where Hemu and his ancestors hailed. Valuable data is available about Sirhind, Narnaul, Alwar, Rewari, Agra and Delhi. Much light is thrown on the then granary of northern India, the prosperity and the subsequent ruin as well as economic depression due to the 1st battle of Panipat, battle of Khanwah and the resultant anarchy. The vicissitudes experienced by the Reis, Zemindars and the elite during 1520 and 1553 can well be imagined. No wonder during this period the once prosperous ancestors of Hemu, residing at Narnaul, Mechari, suffered a set back and migrated to Rewari, when their other relations also lived. Sher Shah also prided in having connections with Narnaul and so did Hemu and his parents. .

According to Babur's own memoirs, when he entered Agra, it was hot season, "All the inhabitants had run away in terror. Neither grain for ourselves nor cane for our horses was to be had." Besides that Babur secured vast treasure at Agra and bestowed lakhs to Humayun, and suitable money-gifts were given to every tribe, there was viz Afghan, Hazara, Arab, Biluch etc., each according to its position. Valuable gifts were also sent to Samarkand and Khurasan. As Agra offered to Babur not only gold, but prospects of founding a new ruling house in India, so he stayed back.

Similarly *Humayun-Nama* of Gulbadan Begum and *Tazkirat-ul-waqiat* of Jauhar give details about Humayun's plight after 1540 A.D., his wanderings, exile in Persia and struggle for reconquest of India. Jauhar began his book in 1587 and his work is of some importance for the reign of Islam Shah, under whom Hemu first rose to eminence. His is an eye-witness account and straight forward, although weak in chronology.

Even *Jehangir-Nama* throws floodlight on various events and aspect of Akbar's reign, his accession to the throne and execution of Hemu. His allusion to Akbar's experiment with Hemu's portrait at Kabul, when only a boy, is interesting. The autobiography also gives a description of the fortress of Mankot.

Masir-i-Rahimi of Abdul Rahim Khan Khana, son of Bairam Khan, throws interesting side-light on Hemu. It was completed by Muhammad Abdul-Baqi Nihavandi in 1616 A.D. It also contains a history of the provincial kingdoms besides a detailed account of Akbar's reign plus a biographical sketch of Bairam Khan.

Tarikh-i-Akbari was written by Muhammad Arif and completed in 1580 A.D. But it is of great value as it offers a view-point independent of Abul Fazl and Nizam-ud-din. It throws some light on Akbar's personality and government.

Tazkira-i-Humayun-wa-Akbar written by Ahmad Yadgar gives interesting account of Akbar's faith in Sufis and Saints. At the suggestion of Bairam Khan, Akbar approached Shaikh Jalal-ud-din of Thanesar and sought his blessing in his conflict with Hemu. The Persian and Turki Divans of Bairam Khan, Khan Khanan, ed. by E. Devison Ress, 1910 and Diwan of Biram Khan ed. by S.H. Rashidi and others, Karachi, 1971 throw light on Bairam Khan's strong disapporval of Akbar's preference for Hindus. The *farman* quoted in full by Abul Fazl, indicting Bairam Khan reveals Akbar's mature mind as a statesman and administrator. It was only after Bairam Khan's dismissal and death that Akbar came of his own in 1562, the most significant year in his life. He abolished enslavement of men and women in war, married a Hindu wife; got pilgrim tax abolished in 1563 followed by abolition of Jaziya in 1564. Over and above these in 1563 A.D. he isued a firman to Hemu's descendents at the behest of Saint Newaldas.

Afghan Chronicles :

By far the most important source in Persian is *Tarikh-i-Sher Shahi* of Abbas Sarwani, which was written at the command of Akbar about 1580 A.D. As he was conected by matrimonial alliance with the family of Sher Shah, his accout of the Sur Kings is of great importance. It contains an account of the early life, of Islam Shah. In order to include certain episodes, such as the history of Baz Bahadur, the Karranis, the Lohanis, Ibrahim Bataim incorporated into the narrative selections from the *Tarikh-i-Nizami* and certain extracts from the account of *Mukhzan-i-Afghana,* thus bringing *Tarikh-i-Sher Shahi* to completion.

Besides *Tarikh-i-Sher Shahi* of Abbas Sarwani, *Waqiat-i-Mushtagi* – by Shaikh Rizqullah Mushtaqi (1492-1581) is of some importance, although it is full of absurd stories. As the author was a religous minded man, he took delight in spirtual exercises.

Tarikh-i-Shahi known also as *Tarikh-i-Salatin-i-Afghana* by Ahmad Yadgar contains a lengthy account of the successors of Islam Shah; but his accounts are not trustworthy. They differ from other narratives e.g. his account of the disturbance in the audience hall of Adil Shah at Gwalior; and the murder or Shujat Khan. The book was completed between the years 1595 and 1613 A.D.

Tarikh-i-Ferishta by Muhammad Qasim Ferishta, is almost identical with that of *Tabaqat-i-Akbari,* However it has own version about the death and execution of Hemu.

Tarikh-i-Daudi was written by Abdullah and translated partly in Elliot and Dowson, Volume IV.

Makhzan-i-Afghana by Neamutullah is a work of great importance, so far as the history of Hemu and His Times is concerned. Severel manuscripts are available and they have been translated by Bernard Dorn, Elliot and Nirodbhushan Roy, Reader, Visva-Bharati, Santiniketan (first volume published in 1958.)

Neamutullah's work is note worthy among the Afghans chronicles on account of the style and quality of narration. This incorporates *Tarikh-i-Khan Jahan* better known as *Makhzan-i-Afghana.* Begun at the instance of the Afghan nobles Khan Jahan Lodi in 1609-1610 A.D., it was concluded in 1613 A.D.

While translating The *Makhzan-i-Afghana* -----Neamuttullah's History of the Afghans, Nirod Bhushan Roy claims to have utilised the Afghan chronicles like *Waqiat-i-Bahari; Tarikh-i-Daudi; Tarikh-Shahi Massir-i-Rahimi, Humayun Namah* etc. in giving annotations. But his labours could only cover the Lodi period and so its importance for the present work is limited.

Neamutullah's narrative is a valuable source of history for the rise and martyrdom of Hemu: Ahmad Yadgar's work entitled *Tarikh-i-Salatin-Afghana* written about 1595 A.D., during Akbar's reign gives details uptil the death of Hemu in 1556 A.D.

Besides these two, Abbas Sarwani's *Tarikh-i-Sher Shahi* and Nirzamddin's *Tabakat-i-Akbari* are equally valuable. The former work was written by the order of the Mughal emperor Akbar. The author bestowed upon it the title "*Tuhfat-i-Akbar*

Shahi" but Ahmad Yadgar who had written the *Tarikh-i-Salatin-i-Afghana*, a few years afterwards, called that the "*Tarikh-i-Sher Shahi*" The exact date of its composition is not given, but it was porbably written after 1579 A.D. Its use was made by subsequent writers, viz. Ahmad Yadgar and Neamutullah, who had acknowledged their obligations. Some light has been thrown on the various translations of the Manuscripts of The *Makhzan-i-Afghana* mentioned by Nirodbhushan Roy, as Dr. Lees Ms. from which Dorn has translated, Sir Jadu Nath Sarkar's Ms. from which Roy has translated only the first volume, covering only the Lodi period. For the present work on Hemu and his Times, it is only of partial importance. Reliance has yet to be placed on Dorn's translation which has given details and Abbas Sarwani's work.

Tarikh-i-Sher Shahi :

Abbas Khan Sarwani, the author of the *Tarikh-i-Sher Shahi*, was the son of Shaikh Ali Sarwani. He was connected by marriage with the family of Sher Shah, and so had peculiar sources of information as to the life and character of that adventurous and successful chief, whose craft and valour won for him a crown. He was granted by Akbar the distinction of the command of 500 horse, but he soon lost that privilege, when he wanted to return to his ancesteral country.

Khan Khanan took pity of him and procured for his a stipend of 200 rupees a month, which he soon lost afterwards. However according to the orders of the Mughal emperor Akbar,he wrote the work *Tarikh-i-Sher Shahi*. According to Sir H. Elliot, "The conclusion of the work containing the regulations is very valuable, though over laudatory. The account which he gives of what the governors did and did not, *shows a fearful state of existing anarchy*. Much of this matter is also given in the *Waki-at-i-Mushtaqi*".

As pointed out by Kalikaranjan Qanungo in the Introduction to *Sher Shah and His Times*, that the accounts recorded by Abul Fazl and Badaoni were supplemented by that of Abbas Sarwani. In the same manner, but "for the old and gossipy Mushtaqi, the oldest contemporary of Sher Shah, who decided to write down his own reminiscences in the eighties of the sixteenth century, much of the history of Sher Shah would never have come to light despite the labours of Abbas and Neamatullah, Abdullah and Ahmad Yadgar." So Abbas Sarwani's work still remains the most important source for the history of Sher Shah and his successors, including Hemu. Details of the Afghan families, which migrated from Roh, are also relevant, as they had spread over the entire Northern India in no time.

When Sultan Bahlol Lodi was faced with opposition from the Chiefs of the North and South, and Delhi was besieged by Sultan Mahmud of Jaunpur, he thought of inviting his own kinsmen from Roh, to strengthen his hands and also relieve them of poverty. He thereafter issued invitations to the Chiefs of the various Afghan tribes, and those who opted to stay in India were given *jagirs* to their full content. Anybody who thought of returning back was to lose his *jagir*. In this way the Surs also, including the grand father of Sher Shah took advantage of the bounty of Sultan Bahlol. This process was continued by Bahlol's successors and even Sher Shah during his rule; with the result that Afghan Chiefs settled down even upto Bihar and Bengal. Their descendents reconciled with the Mughals and the surviving families of such chiefs had their history. To ascertain their activities during Sher Shah, Islam Shah, Adil Shah and consequently Hemu, local sources have to be tapped. They extend from the *parganas* of Haryana, Bajwara and Narnaul in the Punjab to Shahabad in Behar and places in Bengal. History of such chiefs must be recorded to show against whom Hemu had to fight twenty-two battles during the reign of Adil Shah, who preferred to retire to Chunar to lead a retired life.

In the same manner details about the construction of a fort known as "Little Rohtas". on the road of Khorasan to hold in check Kashmir and the country of Ghakkars, have to be ascertained from various source, e.g. *Tarikh-i-Sher Shahi, The Tarikh-i-Daudi*, and and *Makhzan Afghana* by Neamatullah. It is only the last one that mentions the name of Todar Mal Khatri of Lahore as in charge of its construction. The total cost incurred and which had been written on the gate of the fort, is given by the

Tarikh-i-Daudi. Other details about the elephants and horses available to Sher Shah and the total elephants and horses available to Sher Shah and the total number of *parganas* in his empire, with a *Shikdar* to each of them, has been recorded by Abbas Khan Sarwani and confirmed by the author of the *Waki-at-i-Mushtaqi,* the oldest contemporary of Sher Shah.

As most of the works were either written or completed during the reign of Akbar, they have mentioned details of Regulations, collection of revenue, maintenance of roads, serais, intelligence as well as dak service in one breath about the Surs. While Sher Shah ruled from 1540 to 1545, i.e. hardly five years, and Islam Shah remained on the throne for 8 years, 9 months and 7 days, most of the descriptions covered his period also.

Construction of roads, viz., *Sadak-i-Azam* – (G.T. Road) Attock to Sonargaon; Agra to Burhanpur; Agra to Chittor – Jodhpur; Lahore to Multan; building of about 2,500 serais on the road from Bengal to Indus alone and erection of forts and his mausoleum at Sahasram must have taken enormous time or were they all completed during his reign lasting only for 5 years?

Local Sources : In order to identify the battles fought by Hemu the Persian Sources, Mughal as well as Afghan, have to be supplemented by local sources. Roads between Ajmer and Agra as well as Delhi were few and to other places like Bayana, Kalpi Chibramaur' Chunar, Khwaspur Tanda, uncertain and improperly maintained. Similarly the condition of the then forts at Gwalior, Agra, Bayana, Chunar and other places have to be ascertained from local history. Gazetteer of the places come *handy* for the same.

Although Abul Fazl has not given details about the twenty-two battles fought by Hemu against the adversaries, yet they have to be gathered from various sources. Copious details about the battle of Delhi, fought, and won by Hemu have been given by Abul Fazl as well as Badaoni. This was the twenty-third battle. Thereafter the details of the crucial battle of Panipat are available.

Recently G. Khurana, of Kurukeshtra University, has given details about the exact location of the battle of Panipat in his paper presented to the Punjab History Conference in 1978.

Geneological tables supplied by Hemu's descendents have confirmed the respectable descent of his parents and also his nephew Rai Mahipal as well as his sister's son Ramayya. All of them died fighting in the battle of Panipat. So Hemu was not alone in attaining martyrdom.

Scattered information about the forts, which were either captured by Hemu, laid seige to or were of importance has also to be pieced together from local history. It is a pity that very little has been written about the role of Todar Mal in getting the fort of Rohtas built in the Gakkar territory, now in ruins in Pakistan. In the same manner the importance attached to the renowned fort of Chunar has not been properly highlighted. Sher Shah got immense treasure from that fort, and subsequently when Hemu won that for Adil Shah Sur, he was acclaimed as Vikramaditya. Apart from these forts, the Surs, Islam Shah and later on Adil Shah preferred to reside at Gwalior. In view of the danger from the Mughals, Salimgarh fort was built under Islam Shah. What part did Hemu play in getting that built is yet to be ascertained? Archaeological Report have to be counsulted about these and various other forts.

A remarkable publication by Olaf Caroe, the prepartition Lt. Governor of North West Frontier province, entitled *The Pathans,* throws illuminating light on the tribal territory, the forts there and the failure of the first two Mughal emperors of India to have any worthwhile control over them.

European Sources : A number of European travellers, Jesuit priests, merchants and adventurers visited India in the sixteenth and seventeenth centuries. They have left valuable descriptions and narratives as well as their observations. Althogh these accounts cannot always to be accepted as authentic, but on the otherhand they cannot be dismissed as mere gossip. At times these travellers noted what appeared to Indian chroniclers as common place and unworthy of being recorded. To some of the foreigners they appeared to be novel and interesting. As most of such European travellers visited India during Akbar's reign or subsequently, much cannot be gathered from them about Hemu and His Times.

However in this category Travels and Adventures of the Turkish Admiral Sidi 'Ali Rais in India, Afghanistan Central Asia and Persia during the years 1553-1556 is quite important. His account has been translated by A. Vambrey (Luzae & Co. London, 1899), and it throws light on Humayun's last days and his accidental death.

The other important source is De Laet's De Imperio Magni Mogha six India Vera Commentaries ex Varris Auction bus Congestia, Leyden, 1631. It has been translated into English by S.N. Banerjee, under the title *The Empire of the Great Moghal*, Bombay, 1829.

Francois Bernier has recorded his observations in his *Travels in the Moghul Empire*, from 1656 to 1668. They are of limited importance so far as the social and economic conditions go.

According to *the History of Bengal*, Dacca University the Portuguese historians found nothing worth recording during the two decades 1538 to 1558, when they were active in the Eastern Seas and on the Coast of Arracan. In the words of Dr. Qanungo, "This silence about Bengal on the part of Portuguese historians is the best though silent tribute to the strong Pathan regime initiated by Sher Shah."

As most of the period covered by Hemu and the Surs was only an inter-regnum between the Mughal emperors, Babur and Humayun on the one side and Akbar on the other, much details about Hemu and His Times are not available from the Travelogues. Consequently the calumny showered by the Mughal chroniclers on Hemu, and his the so-called low descent could not be counteracted till his community records could be unearthed and Hindi sources tapped.

Geneological Tables : Geneological table of Hemu's family was first of all published by Dharma Mitra, in his booklet "Hemu veer" in Urdu. This was alleged to have been supplied by descendents of Mahipal Rai, the branch headed by Rai Narain Das Bhargava. Prior to the publication of the first edition of Hemu and His Times, the details given by the descendents were tallied with records available in the *Bahis* of Panda Raja Ram of Allahabad, Teerth Purohit of Kaunadia Dhusar Bhargavas. They were found to be reliable. As recognition had been afforded to Nathmal son of Mahipal, a nephew of Hemu, by grant of a firman by Akbar in 1563, so heredity of Hemu was firmly established.

Recently during 1989, the centenary year of the establishment of All-India Bhargava Sabha good many geneological tables of Dhusar Bhargavas of Rewari and other places have been brought ot light. Out of these the most remarkable one is of the anecestors of Ramayya, Ramchandra Bhargava, Hemu's sister's son. This dates back to 970 A.D. This also indicates that when Hemu's father shifted from Narnaul to Rewari, the Dhusar Bhargavas were firmly established at Rewari.

Details about another luminary of Rewari had also come to light, when the first edition of Hemu and His Times, was published in 1961, thirty years back. He was the famous saint -----disciple of Hit Harivansa, founder of Radha Ballabhi Sect at Brindaban, nown as Saint Nawaldas, a cousin of Hemu's father Rai Purandas. Both hailed form Rewari and became disciples of Harivansa at Mathura Brindaban.

Hindi Sources : Fuller details about Saint Newaldas and his connection with Akbar have been recorded by Bhagwat Mudit in his book *Ananya Rasikmal*, which was penned by Dungarsi in 1817. Vikram Era i.e. 1760 A.D. One other Mss. was written down in 1837 V.E. i.e. 1780 A.D. Two such manuscripts are preserved in the library of the Nagari Pracharni Sabha, Varanasi. The former Ms. is from the collection of Maya Shankar Yagnik and the latter is the original collection of the Nagri Pracharni Sabha. In the concluding sentences of the latter Mss. It has been recorded that the same was copied from the original written by Priyadas, for the benefit of Navaneetlal. The work of copying was completed at Brinaban, on the banks of Jamuna, on Tuesday, Chaitra Sudi 2. 1837 Vikram Era. The second one was copied for one Swami Balakdas by Dungarsi in 1817 V.E.

According to Sri Lalita Prasad Purohit, there were several other Mss. copies of *Rasik Ananyamal*, the oldest copy is dated 1789 V.E. He had edited one of them after consulting as many as four other copies of Mss. available with people in Brindaban. There is no vital difference between the five copies consulted by Lalita

Prasad Purohit and he has published the same from Brindaban in 1960 (V.E. 2017). On the basis of his findings the work was written sometime between 1707 and 1720 V.E.

Bhagwat Mudit, the author of the original Mss. was a disciple of Gaudia Sect, but was not indocrinated in Radhaballabhi Sect. His father's name was Sri Madhu Mudit and his teacher was Sri Haridasji. His mention has been made in Canto 198 of Bhaktamal, of Nabhadas and on the basis of notes therein, he was Diwan to the Subadar of Agra, Nawab Shuja-ul-Mulk.

The aforesaid Mss. contains descriptive sketches of several saints and other leading personalities, e.g. Sri Hit Haribans, Hari Ram Vyas of Orcha, Sunderdas, Jaimal, Parmanand, Purandas and Newaldas. These accounts throw a floodlight on the saints and their disciples vis. a vis. their influence on the rulers of the time. However, in context of the present work the descriptive sketches of Saint Newas Das and Parmanand are relevant, for the life and times of Hemu and his father Rai Purandas. In about 207 stanzas Newaldas' devotional aspect has been exhibited on the pattern of Radhaballabhi sect.

It has been also asserted that at the instance of Newaldas that Akbar ordered release of all kinsmen of Hemu belonging to about two hundred families of Rewari. He wanted to offer gift to the saint, but on his refusal to accept any thing Akbar granted a *firman* to Nathmal, son of Mahipal Rai and a grand child of Hemu. According to this *firman* Nathmal was awarded the Qanungoi of Pargana Kanauda in the Sarkar of Narnaul, beginning from the Kharif, dated 8 *Mah-i-Mihr Ilahi,* i.e. 1563 A.D. The *Jagirdars* and *karoris* of that area were instructed not to ask for the renewal of the *firman* every year. Out of the total revenue of the pargana, a sum of 11,000/- per annum was allowed in lieu of the services to be rendered as Qanungo and to cover the salary of soldiers of the Mughal army. The Imperial exchequer was freed from all responsibility of expenditure in connection with that *Mahal.*

The original copy of the *firman*, has been preserved by Sri Suraj Narain Bhargava, grand son of Dharma Mitra Bhargava, author of the booklet "Veer Hemu". Its phot copy has been presented to the National Archives of India, New Delhi, and the experts have deciphered the date of issue as 1563 A.D., i.e. seven years after the battle of Panipat and the death of Hemu.

The relevance and authenticity of Hindi sources has only recently been recognised, and the narrative left by Bhagwat Mudit, himself a Dewan to the Subadar of Agra, should be given due weight. In view of the existence of the original *firman*, the anecdate of Newaldas influencing Akbar, and even giving him *Deeksha, Mala* and *Kanthi*, of Radhaballabhi sect should not be doubted. There might be some exaggeration in the poet's account, but the basic contents of the narrative, i.e. release of all Dhusar Bhargavas, of Hemu's clan of Rewari and grant of a *firman* to his *descendent* have to be accepted.

The enjoyment of the rights under the *firman* by Dhusar Bhargavas of Kanaud, now known as Mahendragarh is supported by records of their families, their geneological tables and other documents. Researches are going on in the history of Mahendragarh, formerly known as Kanaud and it is reported that as any as nineteen *Bastas* ----- entitled *Aibed Nawabi Jhajhar* cover Kanaud. Even Kaushik collection in Haryana State Archives, Chandigarh is expected to contain some related documents about the descendents of Nathmal, the beneficiaries of the *firman*.

— —

Acknowledgements

The Directors of the National Archives of India, New Delhi, and Nehru Memorial Museum and Library, Teenmurti, New Delhi, deserve thanks for having provided necessary facilities for consultation and research. But for that the work could not have been updated and revised thoroughly in incorporate latest researches on the period covered.

Consultation of Hindi Sources, specially the one from Nagri Pracharni Sabha, Varanasi, and its published version from Brindaban, has made the publication of prime importance. Added to them are the various souveneirs and other publications of the All-India Bhargava Sabha, specially during its Centenary Celebrations, in 1989-90. These publications have offorded valuable Geneological Tables relating to the family of Hemu, Mahipal and Ramyya, which should set at rest most of the canjectural theories about the origin of Hemu. The availability of the Firman granted by Akbar to Hemu's descendents, has confirmed the anecdote relating to the meeting of Akbar with Saint Newaldas, described in the Hindi Mss. Ananya Rasikmal by Bhagwat Mudit. Special mention has been made of persons whose contributions have made the work updated and complete in various respects.

I am extremely grateful of Prof. B.R. Grover, distinguished historian for having guided and helped me in revising the work thoroughly and consulting various Periodicals and Journals for researches done on Hemu uptil now.

Sri T.N. Chaturvedi, currently the President of Author's Guild of India, formerly Secretary to the Ministry of Education and Culture, Ministry of Home Affairs and Comptroller and Auditor General of India deserves my utmost thanks for having contributed a Foreword to the work.

Mesers Vishnu Kumar & Bros, Chawri Bazar, Delhi, deserve special mention for having subsidised the publication by providing requisite paper for the same. And Sri S.K. Bhatia, Reliance Publishing House, has done a commmendable task by bringing out the book in record time.

M.L. Bhargava

List of Illustrations

CHAPTER-I

Heredity – birth and parentage

Abul Fazl has categorically stated that after the execution of Hemu in 1556 A.D., Maulana Pir Muhammad, general of the Mughals, "took possession of the Sirkar of Alwar as far as Deoli Sajari (or Sachari), *the birth place of Hemu*".[1]

Birth Place : Deoli or Deoti is in the South of Alwar, and is also known as Macheri or Deoli, where a lake is. It seems to have been one of the chief towns of the district of Alwar in Akbar's time.[2] Macheri is only another name for Sajari or Sachari mentioned by the Mughal historians. It is three miles north-east of Rajgarh. The path between it and Rajgarh is over desolate hills, and was formerly very unsafe. Other important places in this area are Rajpura, Tahla and Nilkanth. The former two have old forts and the latter a few temples.[3] In the *Ain-i-Akbari* these places have been given as Deoti — Sajari. Al-Badaoni has spelled the word as Deoti.[4]

It is clear from various accounts that the region round Deoli or Deoti lake near Macheri, was at one time of considerable importance. It had fortified places and had a host of saints and devotees in temples. The temples at Nilkanth and Bateshwar were of very old reputation. The Shiv Swamis are priests of Narainpur in Bausur, Naldei, a place near Khusalgarh, where Mahadev (Shiv) is said to have manifested himself.

Alwar region in the Mewat tract had yielded a number of Panthis, who disregarded castes and ate together. The Kabir Panthis, Dadu Panthis, Charan Dasis, Ram Snehis, Satnamis, Parnamis, Mohan Panthis all had their ardent followers in the region. Lal Dasis and Charan Dasis flourished most prominently in medieval times. Their founders were born in villages within eight miles of the present city of Alwar.

Lal Das born at Dhaoli Dhub, at the entrance of the Valley of Dehra, four miles north of the city : and Charan Das born at Dehra itself.[5]

Lal Das born of *Meo parents* in 1540 A.D. (1597 V.E.), was though nominally a Muslim, followed the observances of the Hindu religion.[6] Sant Charandas was born on 19 September 1703 A.D. His father was Murlidhar, and mother Kunji Devi. At the time of his birth his grandfather Prayagdas and grandmother Yashoda Devi were also alive. Charandas' grandfather Bhikharidas on mother's side lived in Badarpur, Delhi; while his younger brother Dikherai lived near Baripal. Charandas became famous at Delhi, when Nadirshah invaded the country in 1739 A.D. and thereafter established his *Gaddi* at Charkhewalan.

It is evident from the above that the region of Deoti-Macheri, Dehra were well-known as the abode of saints and seers. Nearby *hillock* known as Dhosi, having a temple was associated with the great Bhrigu Saint Maharishi Chavan; and this place has been claimed by Dhusar Bhargavas as their place of origin. Dhusar word has been derived from this very Dhosi hillock, where at one time Vadhusara river used to flow. The present temple, high upon the *hillock* is accessible after ascending nine hundred steps, and the same is known as "Mandir Dhusaran". The temple has been reclaimed and got renovated, but it is yet to be declared as a tourist spot.[7]

Rewari not birth place : Such was the Mewat region, lying south of Delhi, largely inhabited by Meos and Mewatis, and now extending over parts of the district of Mathura. It formed part of the former Alwar State (now a district of Rajasthan), and a small portion of Bharatpur. Alwar town was its capital. Narnaul was a famous place and in the villages of Macheri were born, the ancestors of Hemu. Rai Jaipaldas was the grand-father and Rai Puranmal was his father. Rai Jhanderao was Hemu's uncle and Jujharrai his brother.[8]

It is clear from contemporary records that neither Hemu nor his father or any of his ancestors were born at Rewari. However from recent investigation about the earliest Bhargava family in Rewari, it has been, revealed that the ancestors of Ramchandra 'Ramayya' Hemu's sister's son, Indrachandra lived there in 970 A.D. They belonged to Kashyapi Gotra and Jakhan (Yakshini) and their profession was agriculture farming and Purohitai. His grandson Srichandra was very learned man and was appointed as Rajya Purohit by Raja Kumarpal of Delhi. He was followed by Budhchand, Mahichand, Arvindchand, Deenchand, in the same position. The privilege was claimed by other members of the family till the reign of Prithviraj Chauhan, with whose fall, the families' importance also declined. In the same family Gunchand was flourishing, when Hemu's sister Punambai was married to him. Out of this wedlock were born the great general Ramayya (Ram Chandra Bhargava) and his brothers Shayam Chand, Krishna Chandra, Mohun Chandra, Hanuchandra, and Ravichandra, most of whom died fighting in the battle of Panipat along with Hemu. In addition two sons of Ramchandra, viz. Mamchand and Parvachand also died fighting. The only survivor was Pushpa-Chand or Pushyarai, born in August 1556 A.D. He was the progenitor of the family thereafter.[9]

Shifted to Rewari : It appears from the subsequent history of Hemu's father that the family seems to have shifted to Rewari. Exact date cannot be ascertained, but the probable date seems to be near about 1525-26 A.D., when the Mughal invasion of India began, and the entire Alwar Sircar, Sirhind and Delhi-Agra regions were disturbed. Fierce battles waged at Panipat and Khanwah. The Afghans suffered defeat and Babar succeeded in founding the Mughal empire in Agra. It was but natural that the finances of the family of Hemu must have suffered a setback, and its members must have shifted from Macheri and Narnaul to Rewari; where they built a house in Qutabpur Mohalla. The site is said to exist even now but is disputed.

On the basis of the above it has been concluded by biographers like Sri Bhagwandev Acharya that Hemu was born at

Rewari, but it is incorrect.[10] Abul Fazl's descriptions based on contemporary investigations are indisputable.

From *Ananya Rasikmal,* by Bhagwat Mudit it is gathered that Hemu's father Puranmal and Newal Kishor Bhargava, both renounced worldly riches and migrated to Brindaban from Rewari, to become disciples of Hit Haribansa founder of Radha Ballabhi sect.[11] The great saint Hit Haribansa after staying sometime at the village of Chirthawal reached Brindaban on *Ekadsi* of *Phalgun,* in 1533 A.D. (1590 V.E.). At that time Humayun was ruling at Agra. Having arrived there he got same beautiful temples built in *Madanter* and established a centre of devotees within a year of his arrival. His fame spread far and wide. Disciples began to enrol from distant places. Amongst the earliest arrivals were Narwahan, Lord of Bhaigon and Newal Das as well as Purandas, from Rewari. Both of them belonged to Dhusar Bhargava caste, and were sincerely devoted to their Guru-Master, who was very much impressed with them and their devotion to Lord Krishna.

Purandas Newaldas deputed : According to the details recorded by Bhagwat Mudit, the author — poet, Purandas and Newaldas were devotees of high order, who had relinquished worldly things. They had become ardent devotees of Radha, Ballabhi Sect. Purandas was deputed to Thatta — in Sindh (now Western Pakistan), where he endeared himself to Raja Parmanand, who has been sent there by Badshah (in all probability Humayun) to look after his interests in distant lands. At first Raja Parmanand held the rank of a three thousand *mansabdar.*

Parandas is said to have reached Thatta in 1535 A.D. (1592 V.E.). Hit Haribansa had deputed him within two years of his arrival at Brindaban. He remained there for about twelve years, when he expressed a desire to return to Brindaban. Bhagwat Mudit has recorded that Raja Parmanand also followed suit, and having profitted by the teachings of Purandas, he lived upto hundred years.

Newaldas and Akbar : Like Purandas, Newaldas, who was his cousin and hailed from Rewari, was deputed by Sri Hit Haribansa to Orcha (Madhya Pradesh) to convert Vyas and he succeeded in his mission. Details of his achievements have been given by Bhagwat Mudit in his *Newaldas ki Katha* (Anecdote relating to Newaldas)[12]. Name and fame of Newaldas spread far and wide and when Akbar went on hunting expedition to Mathura in 1563 A.D., he learnt that the pilgrim had to pay a heavy tax for worshipping their deity there. He considered that as against the pious wishes of the deity he abolished the same throughout his kingdom. His gracious gesture to Hindus was followed by the abolition of *Zeziya* on them. No doubt these two measures were influence by Akbar's matrimonial alliance with a Rajput princess.

Besides the above Akbar was was undergoing a transformation, having being freed from the influence of Bairam Khan and Maham Anaga. He became fond of visiting saints and faqirs in and around Agra — Mathura. Incidentally when he heard about Newaldas' fame he summoned him to his presence. Bhagwat Mudit has related that being of Hemu's caste, Newaldas had been imprisoned, along with other Dhusar Bhargavas of Rewari.

It has been mentioned by Bhagwat Mudit that in the first instance the Mughal soldiers arrested Dhusar Vaish, commonly known as *Dasa Banyas*;[13] but when it was revealed that they did not belong to Hemu's tribe they were let off. Thereafter Dhusar Bhargavas were got arrested and imprisoned. Although exact date of their arrest has not been given, yet according to legends prevailed in the community, they were all arrested after the execution of Sant Purandas, Hemu's father in January 1557. When it was reported that there was only one more left at Brindaban, Newaldas, was also got imprisoned. Subsequently Newaldas, due to his supernatural powers and devotion to Radha Ballabh, got himself freed from prison, in all probability, when after the death of Bairam Khan, Akbar relented, and wanted to meet the saint. But as saints and devotees never tried to play psychophant, Newaldas refused to oblige Akbar. Thereupon he was once more put behind the bars; but he again disappeared as if by miracle.

Akbar and Newaldas.

The Firman ---- from Akbar to Hemu's descendents.

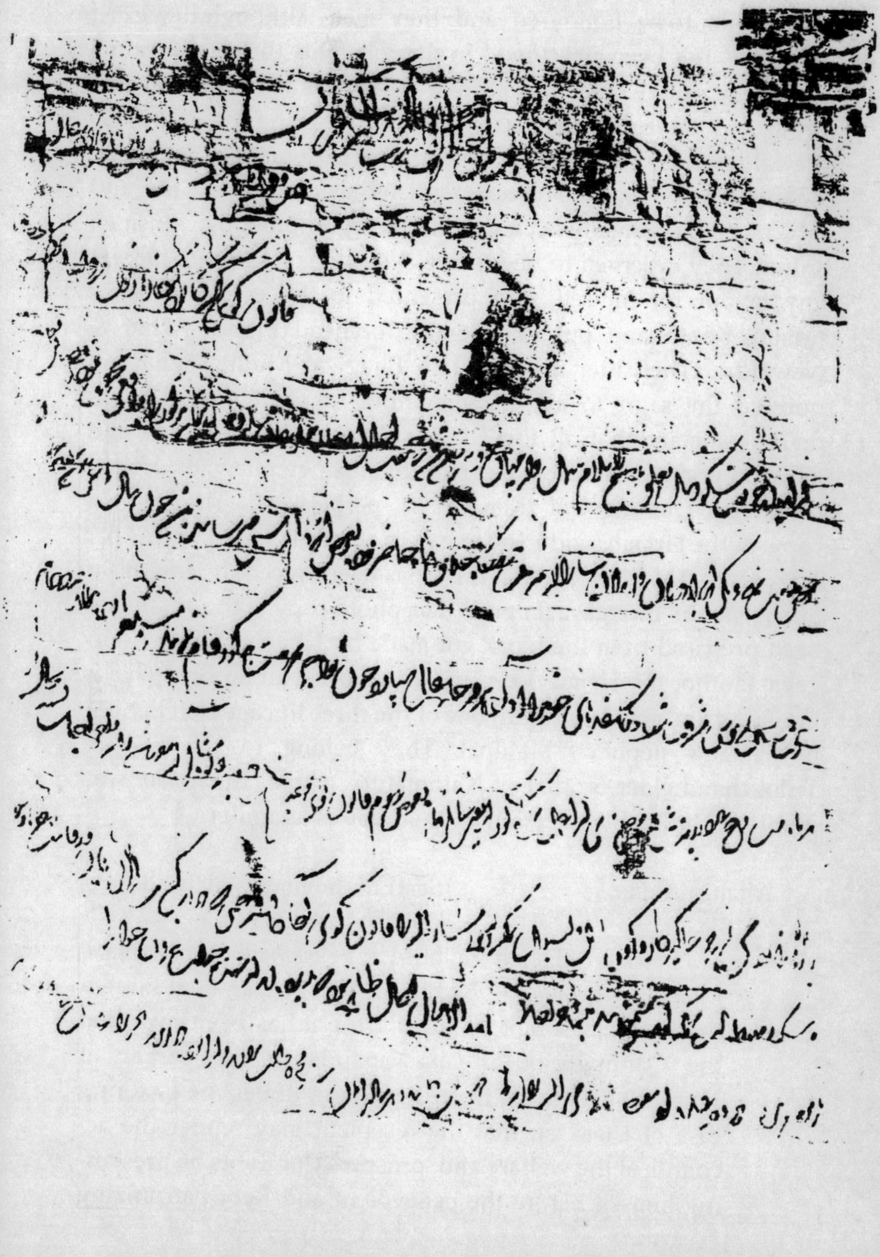

Akbar impressed by the sincere devotion of Newaldas, summoned him to be honoured and they met. Although the exact place has not been mentioned, in all probability the meeting must have taken place in Mathura, when Akbar was already there. This proved to be a momentous meeting, as during the discourse, Newaldas raised the question of the imprisonment of Dhusar Bhargavas of Rewari. He commented that as the real foe and adversary had already been executed, why should his kinsmen suffer. They deserved to be set free. Newaldas refused to accept any favour for himself, and presented to the emperor, beads (Mala), Kanthi and put Tilak on his forehead.(Photo) Akbar & Newaldas. Thereafter according to Bhagwat Mudit, Akbar requested the saint to ask for something for others. And it was on his command that all the Dhusar Bhargavas were set free and a firman granted to Nathmal son of Mahipal, nephew of Hemu, conferring Qanungoi of Kanaur in perpetury.[14] The original copy of the Firman, said to be one of the earliest issued by Akbar on 8 *Mah-i-Mihr Ilahi* in 1563 A.D., has been traced. It is with Sri Suraj Narain Bhargava, Jaipur.[15] The photo copy of the same has been prepared from the block got made by Dharam Mitra Bhargava, author of 'Hemu Veer' in Urdu. Suraj Narain Bhargava is his grandson, and belongs to one of the three lineages left behind by Hemu's nephew, Mahipal. They belong to the line of Trilokchand elder brother of Nathmal to whom the *firman* was granted. The English version of the same is as under :

Allah-o-Akbar (Seal) Mahommed Jalaluddin Akbarshah Ghazi

"Firman Alishan Vajibul-Urz = *Nathmal Wald Mahipal Dhusar dadah shud* = By the Alishan Firman be it known that Nathmal son of Mahipal Dhusar has been awarded the Qanungoi of Purgana Kanauda in the Sarkar of Narnaul, beginning from the Kharif, under the fostering case of Islam; so that the recepient may render the accounts of the welfare and prosperity of Ryots by presenting himself before the benevolent and Ryot patronizing Darbar.

At the end of each year he should honour himself by offering obeisance in the Durbar in person. At the time of thus presenting himself, he should produce all papers in the secretariat of the emperor.

Out of the total revenue of the Purgana, a sum of 11,000/- per annum is allowed in lieu of the services to be rendered as Qanungo and to cover the salary of soldiers of the Imperial army. The Imperial exchequer is free from all responsibility of expenditure in connection with that *mahal*. All present and future *Jagirdars* and *Karoris* of that pargana, keeping in view the Imperial Firman regarding Qanungoi, submit any matter relating to the civil or revenue matter or in the matter of savings or welfare of the public to the above mentioned officer.

The recipient is not required to seek its renewal every year and should never shirk the responsibilities enjoined by the Firman."

N.B. According to National Archives of Delhi's translation, the firman in Khatt-i-diwani bears the *tughra* Firman-i-Jalal-al-din Muhamamd Akbar Padshah Ghazi as well as his seal impression.

As the impression or endorsement on the back of the original Firman has not been photocopied and deciphered, because cloth lining covers that, the endorsement is not available. The owner of the original Firman is being persuaded to get that deciphered and the whole Firman laminated, so that it could be preserved indefinitely.

Hemu's Origin : From the above accounts it should be evident that Hemu did not belong to the Dhusar Vaish community but to a Bhargava family commonly known as Dhusar, tracing their origin to Chavan Rishi, who lived and did penance at Dhosi hill top. This tradition is thousands of years old and the author or *Guru Bhakti-Prakash* has written that the eighteenth saint Charandas of Delhi belonged to Dhusar caste, in which Chavan was born. Even during the time of Mahabharata the hermitage of Chavan Rishi was not very far from Vadhusara river, near Kurukhestra, Haryana. Due to their habitant on the banks of Vasudhara, Bhargavas, tracing their descent from Chavan, came to be known as Dhusars. Vasudhar word became in colloquil language Dhusar only. The present day name of Dhosi village is also a distorted form of Vadhusari.[16]

Not a Baqqal : Al-Badaoni and Abul-Fazl have called Hemu as Baqqal, a grocer, a hawker, a shopkeeper etc., only to denigrade the adversary of Akbar. It all probability it was done to malign a Hindu general and give divinity to the Mughal emperor Akbar. All sorts of ugly epithets have been used against Hemu, whose only fault was, that he was a Hindu challenging the supremacy of Muslims, particularly the Mughal invaders. Hemu's meteoric rise was regarded by both of them as harmful and suicidal for the Muslims, so all sorts of contemptuous phrases and sentences have been used against him. The most conspicuous word that had gained currency during the last four hundred years or more is Baqqal.

Giving an account of Hemu Abul Fazl has exhausted all his vulgar vocalbulary and undignified epithets. He has written, "Let him who searches out the marvels of God's power take a long view and get an instructive warning from the account of Hemu. Outwardly he had neither rank (*hasb*) nor race (nasal) nor beauty of form, (surat) nor noble race (Sairat)". According to the courtier historian Hemu was "evil-looking one of puny form and lofty designs". He was said to have "Ranked among the petty hucksters of Rewari" which was a township of Mewat. He further remarks that for his family (*nasal*), he belonged to the Dhusar tribe, which was according to Abul Fazl, the lowest class of hucksters in India. In his words "At the back of lanes he sold saltpetre (namak-i-shor) with thousands of mortifications (ba bazaran binimaki) till at last by means of astuteness, became a government huckster under Salim Khan, of whom a short account has already been given".[17]

Moslems as Baqqal : The Term 'Baqqal' used by Al-Badaoni and Abul Fazl did not connote any caste or community. It was only a contemptuous term used for the persons, whom the heaven-bern authors deemed necessary to decry. Abul-Fazl has himself described a Muslim general as Baqqal in these words;

Brief account of M. Haidar and his plight due to a schism in the Emperor's army : Khwaji Kilan Beg joined Mirza Kamran, none remained with Haider with the result strife and dissensien resulted in anarchy in Kashmir. Kashmir passed into the possession of the Mirza, but due to Mirza's frigid and insipid bigotries, unanimity and fidelity found a bad market. In 1551 A.D. the Mirza transgressed the law of justice — and took to living for his own lusts and pleasures. The fraud and seditiousness of the Kashmiris again stood up and the hypocritical and wicked faction took the road of deceit and in friendly garb did the work of enemies.

> "Idi Rina and Husain Makri, son of Abdul Makri gained over Khawaja Haji, the Kashmiri Pedlar (Baqqal), who was the manager of the Mirza's affairs."[18]

Here Abul Fazl is describing the faithlessness of the Kashmiri, as their best stroke was separating his capable servants and scattering them by means of strategem. They drew a great many to their side and marched against the Mirza. They also seduced Ghazi Khan and Malik Daulat Caste to desert him. They also made a night attack on the Mirza. He had approached the quarters of Khwaja Haji to release Qara Bahadur, who was a prisoner. Suddenly he lost his life at the hands of Kamal Duhi, though some say one of his own servants unknowingly hit him with an arrow.

According to H. Beveridge Abul Fazl's account of Haider should be compared with Nizamuddin's and Farishtas and also with *Tar Rash.* However here Abul Fazl has described Khwaja Haji as "Baqqal" because he did harm to his hero. A nice parallel to Hemu's being called the same bad abusive name.

Besides the above, there is one more instance of a Muslim being called a "Baqqal" by Al-Badaoni himself when he writes :-

> "On the 10th month the emperor (Akbar) encamped at the town of Romni, (Domini according to *Tabaqat-i-Akbari* — Elliot V, 376) one of the dependencies of Bhojpur, an old halting place. From this place he sent Qasim 'All Khan Baqqal to the Khan Khanan with a view to asking him what he advised to be done..."[19] Yet at another place Al-Badaoni has mentioned one Kalyan Rai

of Gujrat as Baqqal. When Akbar was camping the neighbourhood of Bansala and Dungarpur, Raja Todar Mal brought for him a present of 500 elephants and other valuables. "While at this place Qulij Khan (whom he had recalled from Idar and appointed Asaf Khan as leader of the army in his stead) together with Kalyan Rai Baqqal an inhabitant of Cambay to the port of Surat to obtain an agreement from the Europeans, so as to let free the ships of Sultan Khwajah which for want of such an agreement were lying idle. Afterwards he was to come to Malwah and join the army".[20]

It may be that the meaning of the nick name or colloquial abuse might have different from region to region, but it is evident that Abul Fazl and Al-Badaoni, responsible for the prevalence of this word in relation to Hemu, did not specify his caste or community. It was only meant to decry him and denigrade his achievement by showing, rather highlighting his lowly profession or descent.

Sher Shah's low origin : The Mughals tracing their descent from Taimur had an exaggerated notion of their high lineage. Naturally the court chroniclers praised their masters beyond the realm of reality, and invariably ascribed low origin theories to their opponents. Even Sher Shah according to Abdulla, author of *Tarikh-i-Daudi* was sneered at by Humayun, for being a low-born one. He was, though a king, a commoner and "he yet smelt of a common soldier." The Mughals alleged that Sher Shah's grand father Ibrahim, was a mere *horse-dealer* and hence quite low in rank. It seems that in the eyes of the Mughals, business or trade was the lowliest occupation in comparison to those, who aspired to adopt the profession of "Riyasat" — ruling descent. However, when Sher Shah became a King, it was claimed by his admirers that he was a lineal descendent of the Shamsalam Kings of Gher.[21]

Ferishta also dittoes the same when he remarks in his work, *History of the rise of Mahomedan Power in India,* that "they (Shamshabani's tribe) knew themselves to be descended from the Sultans of Gher. The geneology of Sher Shah according to Abbas Sarwani was as under :-

- Mian Ibrahim
  - Mian Hassan
    - By 1st wife
      - Farid
      - Nizam
    - By 2nd wife
      - Ali
      - Yusuf
    - By 3rd wife
      - Khurram
      - Shadi Khan
    - By 4th wife
      - Sulam
      - Ahmad

Abul Fazl describes Ibrahim as a horse-dealer having no marked distinction amongst the crowds of tradesman. His native country was the village of Shamla in the territory of Narnaul.[22]

This has also been confirmed by *Khulasat-Ut-Tawarikh* in these words :-

"Ibrahim Jodd-i-Farid Yani Sher-Shah Saudagari-e-aspan-we-Kard" (Persian text).

However Mian Ibrahim's son did not take to trade and changed over to the military profession. For a considerable time he lived in the service of Rai Mal the grand-father of Raisal, a Darbari of Akbar and subsequently changed masters.

Hemu's descent : R.C. Majumdar, General Editor of *The Mughal Empire*, Vol. III (Bhavan Series) has written in an Appendix to Sher Shah and His successors that "Hemu was born in a poor family of Dhausar (?) section of Bania caste, being in a town in the Southern part of Alwar".[23] Although Majumdar was writing in 1974, he had not consulted *Hemu's and His Times* published in 1961 written by the author as well as *The Successors of Sher Shah* by Nirod Bhushan Ray in 1934. In both it has been written that Hemu was born in a Bhargava Dhusar family, a sub-caste of Gaur Brahmins. It is a pity that he has repeated without investigation that he was "originally a grocer (or hawker) by profession in a small township in Alwar."[24]

Even Dr. Kalikarajan Qannugo in his *Sher Shah and His Times*, published in 1965 has not done justice to Hemu, when he calls him the son of Ramya of Rewari, who was according to Abul Fazl his nephew, sister's son. Nor was he born at Qutabpur into the Dhusar caste of the Vaish or Bannyas. It is absolutely incorrect to say that they now claim to be Bhargava Brahmin, though still following their original vocation of trade. The Bhargava also known as Dhusar have always claimed themselves to be the descendent of Maharishi Chavan, son of Bhrigu, the progenitor of the Bhargavas.

According to *Skandpurana* the Brahmins, on geographical basis, devided themselves into ten branches, five of them were of the Deccan and the rest five north of the Vindhyas. The latter were known as Saraswat, Gaur, Kanyakubja, Maithil and Utkal. Brahmins residing in the west of begendary Saraswati river, in Punjab and Kashmir were called Saraswat. Others hailing from Kuru and Gud Pradesh, covering the present Haryana state came to be known as Gaur Brahmins, Kanyakubja was the name given to Brahmins of *Kannauj Pradesh*. Residents of Mithila-Bihar were called Maithil, while Orissa Brahmins were called Utkal. Subsequent migrators naturally took these Brahmins to every corner of India.

Under the above circumstances Bhargavas-Dhusar residing in the Haryana, Delhi and Alwar regions came to be known Gaur Brahmins having Bhargava Gotra. Out of these one group amongst them was called *Khan* and the other Dhusar, Dhasia or Dhosiawala.[25] So there should be no loose talk about their having changed their caste nomenclature. Trade and professions were and are even to day secondary.

Thus there is incontrovertible evidence that Hemu, Hemchandra Vikramaditya, son of Saint Purandas,formerly Rai Puran Mal, belonged to Dhusar Bhargava family of respectable status. All low-origin theories and contemptuous references are motivated, false and derogatory. His *gotra* was GALAVA and his *Kuldevi*, Shakra. On the rail-road to Narnaul, eight or ten miles away from Khat Khandole, on the hillock there is a temple of the goddess *Shakra*, which is worshipped even today by applying vermillion with the help of a bamboo (Bans). And according to family traditions he was born on *Ashwin* Shukla Vijaidashmi, 1558 V.E. i.e. 1501 A.D.

Having been born in a comparatively well-to-do land-owner family of Macheri, Hemu inherited all the manly and gentlemanly traditions. His father was a saintly person and having donated all his property to others he started living a life of an ascetic devotee at Brindaban. Hemu's sister Punambai (Purnima Bai) was married to Pandit Gunchandra, a resident of Kutubpur Rewari. Ram Chandra, Ramayya, Hemu's famous nephew was born of this wedlock and had *Kashyapi Gotra*, and *Jakhan* (Yakshni) *Kuldevi.* Ram Chandra had five younger brothers viz. Shayamchand, Krishna Chand, Vishnuchander, Hanuchand and Ravichand.

Notes and References

1. *Akbarnama.*, Vol. II, pp. 71-72.
2. Gazetteer of Alwar, 1878 A.D., p. 164 also Imperial Gazetteer, Vol. III p. 286.
3. Ibid. pp. 164-165 also Tod's Annals and Antiquities Part I pp. 436-439.
4. *Muntakhabut-T-Tawarikh*, Jarrett's translation in English, Vol. II. p. 191.
5. Dixit, Dr. T.N.; *Biography of Sant Charandas* : 1953, also Saint Charandas' historical biography, by Dr. Ramraj Singh, Sri Sant Charandas Bi-centenary of his Nirvana, Souvenir (Smarika), published from Gwalior on 7 December 1982, p. 33.
6. *Gazetteer of Alwur* : 1878 : pp. 164-165.
7. *Souvenir*, Bhargava Local Sabha, Rewari, 1989- Copy of the document relating to Koh-Dhosi or Dhosi Dhaur from Serishta Nizamat Mahendragarh pp. 57-59.
8. Geneological table of Rai Jaipaldas available, having three branches, out of which Mahipal's son Nathmal was granted a firman by Akbar conferring Qanungoi of Kanaud. (Photocopy attached). It has been supplied by the present

descendents of Rai Naraindas brother of Nathmal, living in Rewari.

9. *Bhargava Local Sabha, Rewari, Souvenir*, 1989, Geneological table and history of the earliest Bhargava family of Rewari by Dr. Manhar Gopal Bhargava, pp. 1-7.

10. *Veer Hemu*, Haryana ki Vibhutian, July 1964, pp. 13-14 and page 7.

11. Ed. by Lalita Prasad Parohit, published from Venu Prakashan, Brindaban. Two Mss. copies are available in the MS. Section of the Nagari Pracharni Sabha, Varanasi.

12. Ibid; pp. 15-18, *Ath Shri Navaldas Ji Ki Parichai* also pp. 5-10 for *Ath Shri Vyas Ki Parichai*. According to Lawrence Binyan's Akbar, he was at Mathura for hunting tigers.

13. Ibbetson, Denzil; *Punjab Castes* — 1981 — para 533. The divisions of the Banya Caste — *The Dasa Banyas* are not properly a distinct section of the caste. The words means 'hybrid', and is used for members of other castes who have departed from the custom of the caste or whose descent is not pure. *The Dasa Banyas* are said to be descendents of an illegitimate son of an Aggarwal; p. 244.

14. Ibid. p. 244. The Dhunsars (Caste No. 173). The head-quarters of the Dhunsar are at Rewari in Gurgaon. They take their names from Dhosi, a flat-topped hill near Narnaul, where their ancestor Chavan performed his devotions. They are of Brahmincal origin, as is admitted by the Brahmins themselves, and it is possible that some of them may have recorded themselves as Brahmans in the Schedules. Indeed, I find 1,608 Dhusar Brahmins returned, of whom 1,560 are in Gurdaspur; but whether these are the same men as Dhunsar of Rewari I cannot say... The great Hemu, the leader of the Indian army at the second battle of Panipat, was a Dhunsar of Rewari. Sherring states that the Dhusars have a tradition of origin in the neighbourhood of Banaras (Varanasi) before migrating to Delhi, that they excel as minstrels, and are exceedingly strict Hindus of the Vaishvava sect. They seem to be numerous in the North-west Provinces (now termed a Uttar Pradesh — formerly Hariana,

Ballabhgarh, Delhi also formed part of — the North-west Provinces, Agra); also see *Bhargava Jati Ki-itihas*, by Dr. Purshottam Lal Bhargava, Ch. III pp. 16-17 — The residents of Dhosi were known as Dhusars; and they lived near Vadhusara river, known as Duhan in Haryana.

15. *Calendar of Acquired Documents*, (1359-1754), Vol. II. National Archives of India, New Delhi, 1986 : The Photocopy of the Firman has been examined by the Persian known experts of the National Archives of India, New Delhi. It was also exhibited in the National Integration exhibition, under the head Akbar's Munificence. EKTA brochure 1984 Its text has given the date as 8 *Mah-i-Mihr* Ilahi i.e. 1563 A.D. Certain words have not been properly identified, because of lack of local knowledge and family connections. The Pargana *Kaunar* in Sarkar Narnaul has been spelled as Kanwah, earlier name of Mahendragarh, now a district of Haryana. (Ifran Habib, *An Atlas of the Mughal Empire*, 1982 p. 18) Sarkar Narnaul was transferred to Subah Delhi, sometime before 1655. The Qanungoi of the said purgana was conferred from the *Kharif* crop of Tunquz-II upon Nathmal, wrongly spelled as Hatmal, son of Mahipal and not Chippal or Tharpal. The details have been verified from the family records and geneological tables of Nathmal,'s descendents, who are even today known as *Kanaudias*. The *Bahis* (records) of the Tirth Purohit at Allahabad confirm the same. Another important feature of the Firman was that the Jagirdars and Karoris of the Pargana to whom the Firman is addressed, would release the usage assigned to Nathmal as 'alufa' and not to demand firman and renewal of *Sanad* every year.
16. *Bhargava Jati Ka Itihas*, by Dr. P.L. Bhargava, p. 17. The earliest to throw light on this aspect was Lt. Col. Manoharlal Bhargava in his treatise on Bhargava's history, published in Bhargava Directory.
17. *Akbarnama*, Vol. I. pp. 615-619 : By huckster, be meant a retailer of small wares, a hawker of pedler.
18. Ibid. Vol. I. (H. Beveridge) (1972 ed.) pp. 405-406.

19. *Muntakhabu-T-Tawarikh*, Vol. II. (1986). pp. 181-182).
20. Ibid., Vol. II, p. 249.
21. Banerjee : *Humayun Padshah*, Vol. I, p. 190 fn 2.
22. *Akbarnama*, Vol. I, pp. 326-327.
23. *The Mughal Empire*, pp. 97-101.
24. *Sher Shah and His Times*, pp. 448-449.
25. *Bhargava Jati Ka Itihas*, by Dr. P.L. Bhargava, pp. 15-17.

CHAPTER-II

The Afghan Ascendancy

Afghan historians are unanimous in ascribing the beginning of Afghan ascendancy in northern India to the adventures of Behlol Lodi. His father Kala Lodi son of Malik Bahram of Multan was killed fighting with the Niyaji Afghans during his boyhood. According to the story of Behlol's early life related by the author of *Makhzan-i-Afghana*, the beginning of Behlol's power dates back to his governorship of Sirhind, where he exercised sole power.[1]

At this time Northern India was in a state of political disintegration and the different provinces were governed by petty princes. Anarchy and confusion prevailed alround. Due to internecine warfare, Behlol, as it were, found the crown of Delhi lying on the earth, with his sword and ascended the throne of Delhi on 19 April, 1451 A.D. In the words of Abbas Khan Sarwani, "when Sultan Bahlol, of the family of Sabu-Khail, of the tribe of Lodi Afghan, possessed the throne of Delhi, there were many persons in the various kingdoms of Hind who struck coin, and had the *Khutba* read in their own names and were hostile to him."[2]

Amongst other states, Jaunpur was ruled by Sultan Mahmud bin Sultan Ibrahim Sharki, Malwa was governed by Sultan Mahmud Khilji and Gujarat had Sultan Kutbu-d-din as its ruler. Sultan Alau-ddin Ahmad Shah was in the Deccan and Sultan Zainu-l-abidin in Kashmir. Multan was under Shaikh Yusuf. So long Sultan Behlol remained in the city of Delhi, none of the neighbouring princes dare challenge his might. When he went to help Shaikh Yusuf of Multan and was at Dipalpur, he heard that Sultan Mahmud of Jaunpur had besieged Delhi. At that time he said to his nobles and ministers,

"The countries of Hind are broad and rich, and their Kings are of Indian extraction. In my own land I have many kinsmen renowned for their valour and strength who are pressed for livelihood. *Were they here* they would be relieved from the contempt of poverty, and I could grasp Hind and destroy my enemies."[3]

Behlol got ready response from his Chiefs, who asked him to send letters to the chiefs of the tribes in the Roh country, which he did. On receipt of letters (*farmans*) the Afghans of Roh came, "like ants and locusts, to enter the King's service."[4] He thus initiated a policy which continued to be followed by successive Afghan rulers, including Sher Shah. It was asserted openly that whosoever came to Hind from the country of Roh, was to be given a jagir. If any one of them returned to Roh, his jagir was to be resumed. Consequently although good many of such chiefs returned to their native land, good many of them, who entered Behlol's service, settled down in India from one end to the other in Northern India. Similarly the chief of every tribe and family of Roh came to wait on Sher Shah, and he gave them jagirs far exceeding their expectations. Within a short time the country was full of Afghan tribesmen, who migrated from Roh with their wives and children. The influx gained momentum, with the result that good many Afghan chiefs had become powerful nobles by the time Islam Shah succeeded Sher Shah. Sultan Hussain, King of Jaunpur, ranked foremost among the opponents and adversaries of Sultan Behlol[5]. During his absence in Multan, Sultan Hussain besieged Delhi but his efforts were inadequate, to oppose him and he returned to Jaunpur.

Sher Shah's ancestors : It was under the rule of Behlol that the grandfather of Sher Shah came to India, with his son Mian Hussain, and entered the service of Mian Mehty Khan. According to Abbas Ahmad Sarwani, Ibrahim came from a place called Shargari or Sharghar, or Nasarghari in Afghani dialect commonly known as Rohri, which was a part of Sulaiman Range. It was 6 or 7 *Krohu* in length and was situated on the edge of Kamalpur, near Peshawar.[6] Ibrahim continued in service with Mehty Khan or Mahabat

Khan Sur, who had his jagir in modern Haryana, and Bakhala parganas of the Punjab.

Sometime later Ibrahim broke off his connexion with Mehty Khan and went over to Kemal (Jamali) Khan Sarang Khan, who placed forty horsemen under his command and gave him the perganas Narnaul in jagir. According to Abbas Khan Sarwani, Ibrahim first settled in Baijwara in Haryana. *The Tarikh-i-Khan Jahan Lodi* mentions that he was born in Hisar Firozah, where Ibrahim was serving under Jamali Khan. After evaluating differing evidences Dr. Qannugo had come to the conclusion that Sher Shah remembered "the sleepy *qasba* of Narnaul, which he raised to the status of a fortified district headquarters and where he built a mausoleum over the grave of his grand-father the ruins of which may still be seen there." So he has not found any evidence in favour of the author of the *Makhzan's* assertion that Sher Shah born at Hisar, although *Makhzan* mentions Hasan as *Sakin* (resident) of Narnaul.

Hasan Khan's Vicissitudes : After separating himself from his father Ibrahim, Hassan Khan engaged himself in the service of Qmar-Khan Sarwani, who was one of the leading amirs of Sultan Behlol Lodi.[7] He gave to Hassan a jagir in Shahabad, called Bhowli.

At this very time father of Hemu, Rai Puranmal, born in 1477 A.D. also lived in Narnaul, and continued to reside there during the first few decades of the sixteenth century. It was during this period that Hemu was born in Macheri in 1501 A.D., and was brought up in Narnaul. As the *qasba* of Narnaul was a small one family acquaintances between the Surs and Hemu's father cannot be regarded as improbable. Subsequently visits to the place by Farid were quite natural.

After the death of Ibrahim, Sher Shah's father Hasan petitioned Omar Khan Sarwani, for the conferring of his father's jagir in Narnaul on him. He received the same, and Kemal Khan (Jemal Khan) also agreed to accept him as a vassal.

Transfer of Jemal Khan : Sultan Behlol Lodi's successor Sikandar waged a war against the Sultan of Jaunpur, Berbek Shah, and defeated him. Having done so, in order to strengthen his hold in the Eastern Subahs, Sikander transferred Jemal Khan there, with a force of 12,000 horsemen. Hasan being devoted to Jemal, was asked to accompany him to the East, and was assigned the pergunna of Sahasram with five hundred horse. This included Hajipur and Khaspur Tanda, near present day Varanasi.

Along with Hasan, his family also migrated from Narnaul to the new homeland. There he had eight sons; "two of whom, Fareed and Nizam, were born of an Afghan mother; another consort had brought him Suleman, Ahmed, and Mudaher; and a third one, Ali and Jusuf. The eighth was Shadi Khan, born of a fourth wife."[8] Hasan became exceedingly fond of the last one, a slave girl, and his predication for Suleiman's mother, impaired his affection towards Fareed and Nizam with their mother. In the distribution of estates, he gave one to Suleiman and his brother, in preference to Fareed. This widened the gulf between father and the son, with the result that Fareed independently sought Jamal's patronage and left for Jaunpur.

There has been some controversy regarding the date of birth of Fareed. Abbas Khan Sarwani has made only a vague, statement that "he was born during the time of Behlol", i.e. between 1452 and July 1489. Dr. Parmatma Saran's contention on the basis of *Naqsha-i-Jam-i Jam*, has been discarded by Dr. Qannugo, according to whom Fareed was born in 1486 A.D.[9]

Fareed's early life : From all available sources it is evident that the young Fareed was very much dissatisfied with the conduct of his father, who showed more favours to Suleiman. It is well known in Narnaul and the descedents of Hemu at Rewari that during this period of adversity Fareed and his mother, came to Narnaul and sought shelter with the saintly father of Hemu. This must have been some time between 1501 and 1511 or even earlier. Ultimately he left for Jaunpur. He went there with two fold objects; of prosecuting his studies, as well as securing Jemal's patronage.

Fareed's father Hasan felt perturbed at his son's conduct and fearing its repercussions on Jemal Khan's attitude, he wrote a letter to him to appease his son and send him back for education.[10] Hasan in also reported to have paid a visit to Jemal Khan at Jaunpur.

Exaggerated accounts have been written about Fareed's academic career at Jaunpur, a seat of Islamic learning at that time under the Sharqis. However Dr. Qannugo has rightly concluded that he was some what "sceptical" about the whole affairs, beyond the fact that Fareed acquired a respectable amount of Arabic and Persian learning, read history and the lives of the prophets. Much as also been written about Fareed's vagrancy in Jaunpur. It is evident from his conduct that instead of turning a Maulvi, he was growing as a manly person, fond of brigandage, and art of warfare. .He was very much pained by his own father's arrogance and evil disposition. This lends credence to his readiness to serve other Afghan nobles like Babban Lodi, Nasir Khan Lohani and Taj Khan Sarangh Khan. Consequently he often visited Agra, Narnaul and other places.

Reconciliation : According to Dr. Qannugo, how and when Fareed became reconciled to his father remains a vexed question. It was after several years of his stay for studies at Jaunpur, that on the intervention of some of the Afghan friends of Hasan, that Jemal Khan visited Jaunpur. All of them censured him for putting away so able a son like Fareed to merely please a slave-girl.[11] However accession of Sultan Sikandar's eldest son, Ibrahim, at Delhi in 1517 and danger of civil war, made fortunes at Jaunpur and Sahasram uncertain, and so Hasan felt compelled to entrust the administration of Sahasram to Fareed, as his deputy in January 1518. This alone could enable Hasan to attend upon his master at Jaunpur.

Fareed administered his father's jagir between 1518 and 1522 A.D., which consisted of Sahasram and Khawaspur — Tanda, situated in the modern district of Shahabad in South Bihar. His attitude towards the 'amils, the peasantry and their leaders, the *muqaddams* and patwari's', won for him success and he affected revenue reforms. He dealt with the peasantry firmly and tactfully,but also carried on punitive expeditions against the recalcitrants. But on return from military duties in Jaunpur in 1521 A.D. and due to the intrigues of his step-mother, i.e. Suleiman's mother, Fareed was forced to resign. Upon this both the brothers Fareed and Nizam left for the West and approached Sultan Ibrahim for employment. Thus at the age of thirty-six Fareed was again adrift to begin life a new. According to Dr. Qannugo Fareed left his family in charge of his younger brother, Nizam, at Sahasram. His family between 1511 and 1517 A.D. in all probability consisted of two sons, Jalal Khan and Adil Khan and a daughter. Qutb Khan *alias* Abdur Rashid who was subsequently born pre-deceased his father. He was in all probably born in 1517 A.D., and he was about fifteen years old, when he was surrendered as a hostage and sent under an *ataliq* (guardian tutor) to serve under Humayun in 1532 A.D.[12]

Fareed's Career : The chronology of the period covered by Fareed is very difficult and various. The translator and editor of the MSS — *Tareekh-i-Sher Shahi* has given at the end of his preface a table draw up by H. Elliot, which has not been altered in any way. That differs in some respects from the Table given by Thomas in his *Chronicles of the Pathan Kings.* (p. 393). He has put down the dates — the most trustworthy one are those of Abul-Fazl.

Prior to Ibrahim Lodi's death Fareed had left his father's house a second time. According to Dr. Qannugo this was in 1522 A.D., and there he chose Daulat Khan as patron, one of the three sons of Jamal Khan, Sarang Khan. Fareed tried to procure a royal *farman* for his father's jagir on the ground that his father was too old for service, but he could get that with the help of Daulat Khan only after Mian Hasan's death.

Fareed returned to Sahasram in 1524 A.D. His brother Suleiman, unable to offer any opposition fled. The following year 1525 was a year of turmoil. Babur's incursions had started and the eastern Afghan clans were dismayed. Fareed joined Bihar Khan Lohani's service and earned the title of Sher Khan or 'Tiger Lord' on the occasion of Bihar Khan's coronation as Sultan Muhammad. Every Afghan of some influence received a push upward in rank, title or jagir.[13]

Within a month after Humayun's return from Jaunpur the whole country from Kanauj to Koel in Aligarh was lost to the Mughals except some portion near about Jaunpur. Rival climants of Sahasram usurped authority. Sher Shah entered the service of Babur as a client of *Junaid Barlas,* and received some perganas in the second half of the year 1528 A.D. Sultan *Junaid Barlas* continued to remain his immediate master as the Governor of Sarkar Chunar. Earlier he had been reported to have joined Babur on his Chanderi expedition.

In 1529 Sher Shah is reported to have reluctantly joined the rebels against Babur, but offered submission along with others by 31 March. Got back his jagir finally, after the abortive incursion of Mahmud Lodi in Bihar and his defeat at the hands of Babur. Thereafter ensued worst confusion in Bihar. Sultan Muhammad died and was followed by Jalal Khan a minor, and his mother Dadu acted as the Regent. Jalal-uddin having become a vassal of the Mughal Empire, appointed Sher Shah as Deputy-Governor of Bihar by September 1529 A.D.[14] He continued as such till 1530, when Dudu seems to have died.

Sher Shah and Humayun :

In 1530 A.D. occurred the death of Babur and accession of Humayun took place. Fareed celebrated his second marriage with Gauhar Gossain (widow of Nasir Khan Lohani) and acquired the fortress of Chunar by his marriage with Lad Malka, widow of Taj Khan. Lad Malka was a woman of great sagacity and wisdom and she presented to her new husband rare jewels, pearls and one hundred and fifty *mans* of gold.

In 1531 A.D. Humayun invaded Chunar and forced Sher Shah to come to terms as a vassal. Sultan Mahumad was defeated at Dadrah.

In 1533-36 A.D. Sher Shah consolidated his position in Bihar, and became the King as he emerged as the only hope of the Afghans. He elevated himself to a state of complete independence and no one dared disobey his orders in Bihar.

Sher Shah defeated the Bengal army at Surajgarh. Ibrahim fell fighting and Jelal fled to Sultan Mahmud.[15]

Sultan Mahmud compelled to conclude peace on payment of huge idemnity. Tussle ensued between Humayun and Sher Shah at Chunar and Gaur. Initial victory was of the Mughals, but ultimately Sher Shah celebrated his coronation at Gaur in 1538 and 1539.

In 1539 the battle of Chausa was fought and Humayun escaped.

In 1540 Sher Shah attacked Humayun at Bilgram and defeated the Mughals. This resulted in Humayun's flight to Agra and thence to Lahore. By October end he had to leave Lahore too and remain in exile.[16]

Sher Shah in power

Important events of his region were :

1541 Raided Gaur and took Khizr Khan governor of Bengal a captive.

1542 Invaded Malwa and conquered that.

1543 Invaded Chanderi
Captured Rewari
Invaded Marwar and conquered upper Sind.

1544 November — marched to Kalinjar
Invaded Mewar and captured Chittor

1545 May 22. siege of Kalinjar — Sher Shah fatally wounded by gun-power and dies.

During his rule and Mughals who have been driven out of India could not dare return. Humayun had fled to Sind, Hindal went towards Multan by a different route, and Kamran towards Kabul. Hindal was pursued beyond Chenab, Sher Shah went to Bhera and thence to Khushab where he halted. Humayun was pursued upto Mithankot, and Kamran was driven out by Qutb Khan. At Khushab the Baluch Chiefs Fath Khan, Ismail Khan and Ghazi Khan offered their submission to the Afghan soverign. Sher Shah then launched a campaign against the Gakkars, got a fort constructed with the help of Todarmal Khatri of Lahore, which was got completed by his son Islam Shah.[17]

Sher Shah's policy followed in Bengal, particularly of creating more Zamindaris to make that a second home for the Pathans and replacement of military government by a civilian administration, was relevent for the period covered by Hemu. The whole of Bengal was divided into *Sarkars* by a judicious distribution of the *mahals* and *parganas*. There were 19 Sarkars of Sher Shah's own creation and in Todarmal's Rent — roll they became 24. Sher Shah kept his fingers on the pulse of Bengal and ensured support of the Afghan clans by distribution of zamindaris to them. By building road upto Sonargaon a new terminus for Sher Shah's highway was built up. Hemu in order to keep Afghan's together did not neglect Bengal and made incursions upto Khawaspur Tanda and beyond. Bengal became a refuge for Afghan settlers drawn from all the tribes.

While carrying on his offensive against the Mughals in 1538-39 Sher Shah did not carry on indiscriminate plunder and spared the humble peasantry. "For" Said he "the cultivators are blameless, they submit to those in power." However those who sided with the Mughals were not spared, e.g. the Raja of Arail became the victim of his *wrath* for having helped Humayun's force and was driven to seek the shelter of the wilderness of Bundelkhand, where he earned out an independent principality of Rewa. He also took care that his generals also followed the same instructions.

Dr. Qannugo has very pertinently remarked that Sher Shah opened the country of Bengal to colonization not only by the Afghans but also by the upcountry Rajputs, e.g. Zamindars of Birbhum and Chandrabhan and in Midnapur. And this was the reason why unlike the mughals, the Pathans were not disliked by the Hindu majority as aliens and outsiders. And when their own ascendancy disappeared they took service under the Hindu zamindars and fought against the Mughals to the last ditch. This explains to a great extent that during Adil Shah, when Afghans found their own leaders fighting amongst themselves they readily obeyed Hemu and joined his myriad hordes. They fought against the Mughals and also against Afghan noblemen who were wayward, in as many as twenty-two battles and won victory for their Hindu leader.[19]

On the otherhand much had been written about Sher Shah's guilt in the massacre of Raisin. Abul Fazl and Abbas have uncritically charged Sher Shah with dishonest treaty and promises and taking revenge on survivors. Admad Yadgar has also summed up all the gossip that encampassed the tragic episode. The history of Islam Shah's and Adil Shah's reign affords greater instances of such acts even between the Afghan nobles. The common Afghans felt aghast and so agreed to serve a Hindu general, who could fight against such people.

Sher Shah's conduct against Raja Ramdeo, Maldeo's army with Jeeta and Koopa were all opposed and annihilated as infidels. Neamutullah takes pride in taunting Sher Shah as having punished the infidels. Similarly in the reduction of Chittor, Ranthambhor and Kalinjar, the Mussulmans under Sher Shah's banner, "drew the sword of vengeance, and executed a general carnage upon the whole population." This policy was a departure from the earlier one, when he was considerate for the peasantry. Even at Kalinjar, before Sher Shah breathed his last, he is reported to have demanded total action against Kirat Rai, the Raja of Kalinjar. And when he has been confined to the grave the first act of Islam Shah, on having mounted the throne, was to order his execution. The intelligence of the fort being taken had filled Sher Shah with joy before he breathed his last.[20]

In the words of Dr. Qanungo Sher Shah was "skipping from the crest of one wave of victory to another till he accidentally sank at Kalinjar in May 1545." Had been spared for ten or eleven years more, he would have certainly built an Afghan Empire, leaving no room for the Mughals to return, nor any opportunity to Hemu to show his mettle, as non-pareil Hindu general of the sixteenth century.[21]

Sher Shah's triumphs : Although Sher Shah declared that his war was only against the Mughals, who were regarded as foreign intruders, but subsequently it appears that Sher Shah toed the policy of Behlol Lodi. He was formally proclaimed as King of the Afghans, domiciled in Hind, and invited every Afghan from Roh to come and settle in Hind. Coins were struck and the *Khutba* was read in his name; his appellation of *Khan* was replaced by Shah. He also assumed the title of Shah-Alam. As early as 945 A.H. the coins No. 1257 and 1270 bear the title Sher Shah Al-Sultan. It has been presumed that the *first coronation* of Sher Shah took place in Bengal in the middle of July, 1538 (945 H).[22]

Sher Shah is reported to have assumed the title of Shah before or after the battle of Chausa. However it was only after the battle of Kanauj that Sher Shah's triumph was complete. The Mughals far smaller in number than the Afghans, were badly beaten and massacred. According to Dr. I. Prasad, "Their hearts were not in struggle : They were dispirited, divided and badly led... ... The Hindus seem to have regarded this debacle of Kanauj with complete indifference. There were numerous cheiftains and Zamindars scattered all over the country, but we don't find them ranged on one side or the other :

That the Mughal was still looked upon as a foreigner is borne out by the indifference with which the vast mass of Hindus treated the eclipse of Humayun's fortunes."[23]

The sweeping statement made by Dr. Ishwari Prasad is not substantiated by subsequent fight between Sher Shah and the Rajas of Gwalior, Raisin; Mewar, Ajmer and Marwar. The struggle in Malwa resulted in the death of Sher Shah's youngest son. And in his fight against Raja Maldeo Sher Shah was compelled to seek help from non-Afghans, i.e. Hindus. This is substantiated by number of soldiers involved in the battles between Gaur and Rhohtas in the Gakkar area.

It is on record that Sher Shah found Todarmal Khatri of Lahore as indispensable for the construction of the fort at Rohtas. Sher Shah was furious at Rai Sarang Kakar not waiting on him and congratulating him as all Afghans, from the regions of Roh did and received all sorts of bounties before their departure. Sher Shah is reported to have said that "He would throw such a wedge with the breasts of all the Kakers, that is should stick them till the Day of Resurrection...."[24]

And for that he insisted that the fort might be constructed, whatever its cost; and Todarmal did that. According to the *Tarikh-i-Daudi,* New Rohtas fort cost eight *Krors,* five *lacs,* five thousand and two and a half *dams* which meant Bahlolis. This was got written over the gate of the fort. Its ruins, lie in the district and *tahsil* of Jhelum, situated ten miles north-west of Jhelum town. This could be completed only after Shah Shah's death, when Islam shah had ascended the throne. This practice of mobilising the talent of Hindus was continued by Islam Shah also, after Sher Shah's death. If Todarmal was Sher Shah's discovery, Hemu was that of Islam Shah:

Barmazid or Brahmditya Gaur

As pointed out by Dr. Qanuago Barmazid or Brahimjit Gaur was in all probability one of the Rajput zamindars of the Mungir district, who came over to Sher Shah. The rulers of Kanauj are reported to have fought with the Gaurs of Mungir. And when Sher Shah raised Rajput troops from Bhojpur, they were perhaps commanded by Brahmajit. Dr. Qanungo has discounted the theory of Prof. Hodwala that Brahmajit was an Afghan name. According to him, had he been a Muslim, Badaoni would not have called him an arch-enemy of Islam.

Sher Shah appointed Brahimjit as the Faujdar of Ajmer. It is learnt from the *Mukhzan* that Brahimjit Gaur managed to retain Ajmer, during the region of Islam Shah by deserting the side of Khwas Khan. His career shows that Sher Shah trusted him to a degree to which he could not trust any Afghan.[25]

Whenever it suited him Sher Shah mobilised the Rajpoots for his army. According to Abbas Khan the army that he marched against Raja Maldeo, Nagor, Ajmer and Jodhpur, "the host of the Rajputs could have been scarcely less, if we are to believe the extravagent statement of the *Makhazani-Afghani,* which sets it down at 50,000 cavalry and 300,000 infantry." As the said work was written in the reign of Akbar, it suited the author to paint Sher Shah as fighting against infidel Maldeo and having taken pride in cleansing the country from the contamination of the unbelievers.

Obviously there are two exaggerated accounts about Sher Shah, the first one relates to the expulsion of the Mughals from Hind. Gul-badan has given vivid description of Humayun's flight in these words :-

"His Majesty alighted in Khwaja Ghazi garden near Bibi Haj-taj. Every day there was news of Sher Khan; and during the three month that the Emperor was in Lahore, was brought day after day : *Sher Khan has advanced four miles* — Six miles, till he was near Sirhind. At this time His Majesty appointed Mirza Haidar to take Kashmir. Meantime, news was brought that Sher Khan was there. A wonderful confusion followed, and the Emperor decided to march off the next morning... ...After a weary journey, they reached Bakkar at last."[26]

Sher Shah pursued the Mughals till they were out of the boundaries of Hind. Even Kamran, who was negotiating with Afghans was driven out of Hind till he crossed Indus. According to the narrative in *Khulasat-ul-Tawarikh,* by Sujan Rai, Kamran hoped to obtain Lahore in addition to Kabul. However in accordance with another Persian *Taskirat-us-Salatin* by Muhammad Hadi Kaowar Khan, Kamran spoke thus : "If I be given the Punjab in token of friendship. I shall do such deeds that none would dare be hostile to him." (Sher Shah). He was not prepared to leave the Punjab either for Kamran or Humayun. His simple reply was, : "I have left you Kabul. You should go there." In pursuit of this aim he pursued the Mughals till they were out of the boundaries of Hind. According to Gul-Badan it was like the day of Resurrection, when 200,000 souls left Lahore in flight; overtax of all sources.

The second account is about campaigns against the Rajputs of Jodhpur, Ajmer, Abu, Jalor and other forts. By his devices Sher Shah confounded the Rajputs, kept the Afghans in the alert and under arms, till they forced victory. Different accounts are available in Rajput sources, e.g. Nainsi's *Khyat*, and Muslim chronicles like the *Makhzan*. After the fall of Raisin in June 1543 A.D. Sher Shah started military preparations in an unprecedented manner in Agra and Delhi. Within scarcely four months an army of eighty thousand horse, in addition to infantry, artillery, war elephants and possibly in camel corps, was ready for campaign in Marwar. All chronicles throw light on Sher Shah's marvellous feat of mobilising so vast an army almost at a month's notice.[27]

Sher Shah visited Delhi in September 1543 to visit the new city which was nearing completion and also made 'hunting excursions' through Haryana as far as his ancestral home of Narnaul where he had begun building a fort and a mausolum over the tomb of his grandfather. It was from the direction of Narnaul that the countless army of Sher Shah burst upon Maldev's territory across Shekhewati in the autumn of 1543 (950 A.H.)

Within a year's time Marwar and Mewar had been humbled. Maharana Udai Singh took shelter in the Bhil country of pargana

Jutra, Sher Shah constituted Chitor and its dependencies into a new Sarkar of Chitor, to be administered by Ahmed Khan Sarwani and Husain Khan Khilji under command of Khawas Khan's brother Shamo Khan. In the words of Dr. Qanungo, "Thus after about ten months the invasion of Marwar with its sequel, the subjugation of the rest of Rajputana, came to a brilliant close."[28]

And with that all hopes of Humayun seeking help from Maldev or any other Rajput king of importance disappeared; and he had to leave the frontier of Hind.

Islam Shah

Accidental death, prevented Sher Shah from nominating a successor of his choice. Neither his elder son Adil, nor his younger son Jalal Khan was with him at Kalinjar. The former was at Ranthambhor and Jalal Khan was at Rewa which was nearer to Kalinjar.

According to *The Makhzan* Isa Khan, Khan Gukboor Jemal Khan, and Sheikh Mohammed Gukboor, all influential men assembled to have consultations upon the accession. Isa Khan delivered his opinion in favour of Jelal Khan. According to him Adil Khan was "so addicted to play, gaming, luxury, and amusements" that he neglected even his own concerns and estates. On the other hand, although Jelal Khan's disposition was too rancorous and feeble, he was brave and "the favourite of fortune." He was firmly of opinion that Adil Khan, being too luxurious and lazy, could not conduct the state affairs properly. Jelal Khan, according to Isa Khan, was an illustrious warrior, and had always managed every business, excellently confided to him by Sher Shah. Moreover time was a great factor and Jelal Khan being nearer could assume administration quickly. Moreover it was asserted that the welfare of the Afghan empire could be provided for, by raising the standards of Jelal Khan, and resorting to the shadow of his protection.[29]

As Jelal Khan was only 50 miles away, he reached the place of death in three days. Adil Khan was 200 miles away, but his son Mahmood Khan was at hand. So after obtaining Isa Khan's full consent the Afghan nobles present there drew up two letters; the one addressed to Jelal Khan; the other to Adil Khan. The letter addressed to the letter was delivered to his son, to be conveyed to him. By this pretext, Mahmood was also removed from the camp, before he could learn the truth. In the letter to Jelal Khan it was conveyed that all the Afghan Qmras of his father "anxiously awaited to him, in order to assign the throne to him."

At the outset Jelal Khan hesitated to accept the offer, as that he might antagonize the army. But then all the Afghan grandees had actually agreed on that point, he was ready to take upon himself important affairs. He announced that he was determined strictly to "observe his father's institutions and regulations, without allowing himself the least deviation, but promoting the public welfare."

After his formal announcement Islam Shah made his entrance into Agra at propitious hour and proclaimed himself as Islam Shah, the emperor. Isa Khan, who had been Tenbuldar (betel-bearer) to Sher Shah gained the upperhand.[30]

According to the Makhzan all the Qmras and officers of the Afghan Kingdom, congratulated Islam Shah, the only exception being his elder brother Adil Khan, for when he learned of the whole transaction, he bitterly repented of his backwardness, which, however, served only to enhance his consternation and remorse.[31]

According to Abul Fazl, Sher Shah did not hold any of his sons in high esteem, "one was a luxurious proofligate, fond of ease and pleasure, and the other had a headstrong and vindictive temper."[32] Dr. Ishwari Prasad had gone to the extent of asserting that Islam Shah, "surpassed even his father in wickedness" and was "tyrannuos, mischief maker."[33]

Whilst Sher Shah ruled with active aid and willing co-operation of his kinsmen, Afghan nobles and rewarded them fully, so much so that by the time of his accidental death, they had become all powerful. Islam Shah was led away by one group of grandees, Qmras headed by Isa Khan Hajah while others like Khwas Khan and Isa Khan Niazi, who were posted in Marwar and were nearer to Adil Khan became objects of suspicious. Although in the beginning Islam Shah hesitated to sidetrack his elder brother's claim, but once in power, he wanted to win over all Qmras to his side. So he, on Khwas Khan's arrival at Agra showed his joy and accounced that he had joined him. It was only after he expressed his desire to ascertain the sentiments of Adil Khan and despatched letters to that effect. Several stories have been narrated about the meeting with the two brothers, and according to the Makhzan, when the matter was settled, Adil Khan, accompanied by Khwas khan and Isa Khan Niazi was to reside in Sikandra, and the fort of Bayana, which fort was to be held by Adil Khan. After this settlement no adversary remained throughout Hind and Islam Shah, could reign with insolence and pride. The Afghan accendancy was at its zenith.

Notes and References

1. Neamutullah, *Makhzan-i-Afghana*, trs. Dorn-History of the Afghans, First Book, pp. 43-44.
2. *Tarikh-i-Sher Shahi*, p. 15. (1957 ed.).
3-4. Ibid. pp. 15-16 : According to Riaz Ulmuhabbat, Roh was the name of the country of the Afghans extending on the West as far as the Hemen river, contiguous to the Herat; in the North, as far as Sharghar; on the South to the Barohi Baluchistan; on the East to Kashmir. The inhabitants came to be known as Rohillas.
5. Neamutullah, Book the Second; p. 80.
6. Roy, Nirodbhusan; Neamut Ullah's *Makhzan-i-Afghana — History of the Afghans*, p. 69 : also *Humayun*, by Dr. Ishwari Prasad, p. 96. fn.
7. Dr. I. Prasad, *Humayun*, p. 96; "Not long after the birth of his eldest son, it seems, Mian Hasan Khan Sarwani, a high noble of Behlol's Court, who bore the title of Khan-i-Azam Umarkhan was made Governor of Lahore by the Sultan and given Zagirs in Sirhind.
8. Neemutullah; p. 81; Geneological table of Mian Ibrahim at p. 19.
9. *Sher Shah and His Times*, pp. 24-28 (1965 ed.)
10. Neamutullah : pp. 81-82.

11. *Sher Shah and His Times*, pp. 38-41.
12. Ibid., pp. 57-59; and 38 : also Neamutullah -pp. 82-87.
13. Ibid., pp. 66-71.
14. Ibid., pp. 89-90.
15. *The Mughal Empire*, Bhavan Series, Vol. III, J.N. Chaudhari, pp. 71-73, Dr. Qannugo quoted, pp. 142-144.
16. *Sher Shah and His Times*, pp. 227-237.
17. Neamutullah., p. 131 and *Sher and His Times*, pp. 284-285.
18. Ibid., pp. 254-255.
19. Ibid., pp. 321.
20. Neámutullah, pp. 140-142.
21. *Sher Shah and His Times.*, p. 433.
22. Ibid., p. 190 Appendix to Chapter VIII. Also Dr. I. Prasad : *Humayun*, pp. 137. Abbas supported by Ahmad Yadgar and abdulla assert that it was after Chausa that Sher Shah crowned himself with the consent of the Afghans and adopted the insignia of royalty.
23. *Humayun* : pp. 145 and 155.
24. Neamutullah, p. 1131.
    Sher Shah and His Times, pp. 284-285.
    Abbas Khan Sarwani, pp. 142 and fn. 105.
25. *Sher Shah and His Times*, pp. 411-418 and 420-421.
    Appendix to Chapter XVII. Same facts relating to Barmazid.
26. *Humayun-Nama*, trs. Beverdge, pp. 140-147.
27. *Sher Shah and His Times*, p. 392.
28. Ibid., 416.
29. Neamutullah, pp. 142-143.
30. Ibid., p. 146.
31. Ibid.
32. *Ain-i-Akbari*, Jarett-II. pp. 159-160.
33. *Humayun;* p. 181.

CHAPTER-III

Rise of Hemu

Widely different versions have come down abut the meteoric rise of Hemu. Unfortunately the courtier historian Abul Fazl, had poured all venom on his soverign's adversary. According to him Hemu rose to power, during the reign of Islam Shah, but in his words he only became a government huckster under Salim Khan (Islam Shah) and that too by means of his astuteness. Abul Fazl has neither specified any reason for Salim Khan's choice of a Hindu as his minister, or a high administrative officer, nor given any date of his assumption of power.

> He has only recorded that "By master-piece of feline trickery, he *gradually* made himself known to Salim Khan by evil speaking and business capacity. He was always bringing people into trouble. Apparently he was behaving loyally towards his master, in reality he was seeking his own ends, and decking his own household, with the goods of the oppressed."[1]

Abul Fazl has admitted that Hemu soon got a place in Salim Khan's affections by mis-representations, "and obtained a footing in the administration." It is not clear from his prejudicial account, why and how Islam Shah, took fancy to him and gave him precedence in administration over his Afghan nobles. Was it due to Hemu's extraordinary administrative powers or due to his family status and influence at Delhi, coming as he did from Rewari having links at Narnaul. Abul Fazl's lefthanded compliments to Hemu only show that he has called him *huckster*, etc. because of his being the foe of Akbar and a Hindu. Although

Abul Fazl had made searching investigations about Hemu's birth place, family and his father he had not bothered to narrate the causes of Hemu's alliance with Salim khan, who is better known as Islam Shah. Badaoni has also mentioned Islam Shah as Salim Shah. [2]

It is often forgotten that Sher Shah was born at Narnaul, and his children were born between 1508 and 1517, when he was at Jaunpur. Jelal Khan had two brothers, one Adil Khan who was elder to him and the younger one was Qutb Khan. The youngest predeceased his father. However it is on record that during their boyhood Sher Shah was a frequent visitor to Narnaul, where Hemu's parents also lived. Contacts between Sherhah's children and Hemu are quite probable. Hemu was born in 1501 A.D. and so he must have been only a few years elder to Islam Shah. According to the details culled from Hemu's family sources at Rewari, late Major Manohar Lal Bhargava has written that Hemu belonging to Rewari, was reintroduced to Islam Shah by a Modi(official business man) at Delhi. It was on his recommendation that he was appointed as Superintendent of the Market, and subsequently rose to be a Minister for Food and Civil Supplies under Islam Shah Sur

Hemu's apprenticeship: Although Hemu's family hailed from Narnaul, but it appears from family records that during the period 1526 and 1545, due to frequent wars, famines, there had been some migrations. In all probability Hemu's family migrated to Rewari during this period and his saintly father took to Bhakti cult in Mathura — Brindaban as a disciple of Hit Haribansa, the founder of Radha Ballabh. sect, at Brindaban about 1535 A.D.

This was the worst time in India's history, as the battles fought by Babur and the Pathans, resulted in worst anarchy. Humayun had to face the turbulance, uncertainty, and challenges alround. In such a time Hemu's family must have naturally shifted from Narnaul to Rewari, where his relations on maternal side lived. Departure of Hemu's father to Brindaban and then his deputation to Thatta to preach Radhaballabhi teachings, resulted in a setback to family's finances.

The Marwar campaign occupied Sher Shah's army for not less than six long months i.e. till the beginning of May 1544. Narnaul, which was a *pargana* of Hisar Firuza down to the end of the Lodi Sultanate, was constituted by Sher Shah into a *Sarkar*.[3] At the start of the campaign Sher Shah's armies gathered at Narnaul and Agra and the whole area was in ferment during that period. Anarchy was inevitable.

It is obvious from all contemporary accounts that during 1535 and 1544 residents living in Mewat, Rewari, Narnaul and nearby places had to witness mass mobilisation of armies and movement of troops. Rajputs and Mewatis along with other residents had no option but to arm themselves. Naturally Hemu who was in the prime of youth during this period must have undergone training in warfare and gained experience of the preliminaries of mobilization, elephant warfare and Pathan mode of fighting.

According to Abbas Khan Sarwani, "Sher Shah always kept 1,50,000 horse and 25,000 footmen, either armed with matchlocks or bows present with him, and on some expeditions took even more with him."[4] His whole army, when mobilised was beyond all limit or numbering, and it increased everyday. And in each fort he kept a force, with matchlockmen attached to that. In the fort of Rohtas (Bihar) 10,000 matchlockmen were kept. The *Tarikh-i-Daudi* mentions that he kept 8,000 matchlockmen in his service. Besides the above there were 5,000 elephants in his sheds, some of whom were trained for warfare. In order to maintain such a huge army Sher Shah kept treasures in various forts, the biggest was in Rohtas.[5]

Islam Shah's zeal : Having ascended the throne in the absence of his elder brother Adil Khan, Islam Khan started wooing the four powerful nobles. Khawas Khan was conciliated by him. Qutb Khan *Naib,* Isa Khan Niazi and Jalal Khan *bin* Jalu were selected to go and bring Adil Khan to the durbar. Jalal Khan advised Islam Khan to march to Ranthambhor and drive away his brother beyond the limits of the Sur Kingdom. But Shah Muhammad Farmuli advised moderation and favoured bringing Adil Khan from Ranthambhor in good faith to prevent a Civil War.

Islam Shah tried to maintain strict discipline in the army and took that into confidence. He expressed his readiness to reward them as his father used to do. He continued the espionage system in proper trim. Although Islam shah was very liberal and magniuimous in rewarding the military nobility, no one trusted him because of his espionage system. the spies were required to report regarding the doings of the highest dignatories. According to Dr. Qanungo, on the occasion of the first meeting with Adil Khan, Islam Shah had planned his murder, by secretly instructing the guards to keep out the followers the three nobles siding with him. The plot failed as their partisans, suspecting foul play, forced themselves into the audience hall.[6]

Conflict with Adil Khan : 1546 A.D. while the leading nobles were busy winning favour of Islam Shah, Prince Adil Khan "... bitterly repented of his backwardness, which, however, served only to enhance his and consternation and remorse."[7] Accordingly Adil Khan deputed his son, Mahmood Khan, to Agra, to reduce it, but the nobles did not endorse his action and he was forced to retreat in utter disappointment. Even Khawas Khan could not support Adil Khan's candidature for the throne and Islam Shah, showed all symptons of joy at his conduct. After having claimed his accession Islam Shah proclaimed that he was desirous of reconciling to his brother, if he was "inclined to banish all rancour from his mind, and to co-operate in removing their reciprocal animosity and disaffection."[8] It was agreed that Adil Khan might be approached to show his sentiments.

When Adil Khan received letters from leading nobles, he sent a message to Islam Shah that Khawas Khan, Qutb Khan Sur and Jelal Khan might be empowered to pacify his apprehension, so that he could present himself in the durbar. Islam Shah was anxious that Adil Khan might be ousted from the fort of Ranthambhor and he wanted to bestow upon him the fort of Bayana instead.

On being assured by the three nobles sent to him, Adil Khan handed over the keys of the fort of Ranthambhor to the deputies of Islam Shah. The two brothers are reported to have met at Khano, in the vicinity of Shikarpur. Those are several anecdotes current about what transpired at that place. However, ultimately Islam Khan obtained consent of Adil Khan for his accession and deputed Khawas Khan and Isa Khan Niazi to accompany him to Sikandur, at the fort of Bayana, which was no be held by him, as a jagir.

In this way the conflict with his elder brother was resolved and Islam Shah became very proud and insolent. But even after that he reasoned that so long as Adil Khan remained alive, "there would be something to fear and apprehend for the throne."[9]. So Islam Shah, shortly after deputed Ghazi Khan to go to Bayana, and bring Adil Khan to the court at Agra in chains. When Adil Khan learnt of that he consulted Khawas Khan and Isa Khan, who advised him to either gird up the sword or go in chains to the court. They felt convinced that Islam Shah had committed a breach of the terms agreed upon. Having obtained help from other nobles, Khawas Khan decided to advance towards Agra, "to commence hostilities against Islam Shah".[10]

As soon as Islam Shah learnt of the imprisonment of Ghazi Khan, his emissary and open revolt of Adil Khan, he tactfully took the nobles into confidence. Having failed to appease all, Islam Shah prepared to fight. When the rebels advanced upon Agra, in full pride, on the twenty-seventh of the month of *Ramzan*, Islam Shah came out of the citadel to charge upon the insurgents. Bitter fight ensued, but Adil Khan when repulsed, "fled and abandoned his troops to a complete rout." According to *The Makhzan*, he crossed the Jamuna (Yamuna), and reached Chandwar, and continued his flight to Patna.[11] Islam Shah was very much overjoyed at his victory and rewarded his followers, both the faithful and those who had been incited to rebel, by promotion. Only Khawas Khan and Isa Khan managed to escape to Sirhind, Jalal Khan *bin* Jalu, Brahmjit Gaur and a few others left the side of Khawas Khan in disgust and joined Islam Shah.

Battle of Ambala: 1547 A.D. The whole Afghan nobility was in ferment. Most of the nobles felt scandalised at the conduct of Islam Shah against his elder brother. But Islam Shah persisted and a decisive battle took place in 1547 A.D. against the Niazis under Haibat Khan. Khawas Khan, who had taken shelter in the

Kumaon hills, thinking that the Niazis were fighting for the cause of Adil Khan, came to fight Islam Shah. But when he learnt that the powerful Niazis were out to establish their own hegemony, Khawas Khan withdrew from the battle of Ambala. As a result of his desertion the Niazis broke and fled, suffering heavy casualities. Haibat Khan drove towards the Salt Range and joined the Gakkars. After the victory, Islam Shah returned to Agra and thence proceeded to Gwalior.

Conquest of the Gakkar territory : 1548-50 A.D. Islam Shah was determined to root out the powerful Niazis and so he raised a grand army in Punjab. As he had become suspicious of the Afghan nobility, he raised a large number of Hindu troops, mainly infantry, to overawe them.[12] Islam Shah like his father, had a keen eye for military strategy, and so decided to build forts of Mankot, Rashidkot etc. for the defence of Punjab. He had already allowed Todarmal of Lahore to complete the fort of Rohtas, even after the death of his father and later on on he harnessed the services of Hemu also to fight his adversaries in the Punjab. For full two years Islam Shah was busy in Punjab and got forts and towns built at Mankot. In Delhi he also got erected a mausoleum in his garden for the two Lodi Sovereigns, Behlol Lodi and Sikandar Lodi.

The Gakkars were compelled to drive away the Niazis from their territory, as Islam Shah pursued the campaign against Haibat Khan to the bitter end. It did not worry him that Haibat Khan Niazi was at one time faithful general of his father. The Niazis were hunted out of Punjab and Kashmir. The Gakkar driven to hunger and privation by destruction of cattle and vegetation, were forced to surrender. Islam Shah killed every morning some Gakkar captives to overawe them and returned to Agra. Weakened and reduced to distress by continued slaughter and desolation of their lands the Gakkars left their country for the mountains in Kashmir.

Hemu in Punjab : Hemu was holding important post of Superintendent of the market of Delhi, when Islam Shah started his campaign against the Niazis. Subsequently he was also made Superintendent of Posts and Chief of Intelligence. Both were very vital to Islam Shah's ruthless campaign in the North-West. Islam Shah quickly "discovered soldierly qualities in him and raised him to the position which Brahmjit Gaur had held under Sher Shah". In Dr. Qanungo's words, "In conformity with his policy of always placing a Hindu in command alongside and Afghan officer to spy on one another, Islam Shah sent the contingent of Hemu along with others to watch the movements of Kamran Mirza, miserable and blinded, coming to his court in the neighbourhood of Mankot."[13]

Kamran's distress : When Humayun succeeded in conquering Kabul from his brother Mirza Kamran, the latter was forced to flee and seek help as well as protection from Islam Shah, March 1552 A.D. In actuality when Kamran met Islam Shah he was humiliated, as he was required to perform the customary salutation.

On the extinction of the Niazi rebellion, Islam Shah took Kamran in his custody to Delhi, but on way he fled, disguised as a woman. Consequently he was again imprisoned and handed over to his brother Humayun, who caused him to be blinded. During this incident Hemu, who had risen to eminence under Islam Shah was deputed to escort Mirza Kamran to his presence.[14]

With the death of the Niazi leaders, Islam Shah was freed from anxiety for sometime. During 1550-1551 he established friendly relations with Mirza Haider, the ruler of Kashmir. While staying at Delhi, Islam Shah decided to strengthen the defences against the return invasion of the fugitive Mughal emperor, Humayun. It was at this time that he laid the foundation of the fortress of Salimgarh on a hilly rock, north of the present Red Fort, and on the bank of Jamuna. Its ruins can even now he seen near the old Delhi railway station. Entrance to it is from the Red Fort end but it is a still prohibited area.[15]

It is not clear from the scanty records of the time, who supervised the construction of the fortress of Salimgarh. Islam Shah feeling safe left the control of Delhi to Hemu, his able minister, incharge of civil and military affairs, and "returned to Gwalior, and freely indulged in the pleasures of the chase."

The Afghan nobility finding Islam Shah, revelling made a second attempt on his life at Antri-Fort.[16]. The plot was soon discovered and Islam Shah reached the capital by a different route. He seized upon the conspirators and put them to death, including Bahauddin Mahmud and Mada.

Last days : Busy in pleasure and enjoyment Islam Shah had become afflicted by painful desease, a tumour in his privy parts. There are other versions too about his disease, and about his undergoing treatment with leaches. He passed away on October, 30, 1553, and his body was removed from Gwalior to Sahasram, and buried not far from the tomb of Sher Shah, his father. There are several versions about the date of his death. Nizamuddin and Ferishta mention that he died in the beginning of 960 A.H. Abdullah gives the date only as 960 A.H. Abul Fazl places it on 22nd Ziqada 960, i.e., October 30, 1553 A.D. which is widely accepted date.

Islam Shah and Hemu : According to Al-Badaoni, Islam Shah had begun to repose so much faith in Hemu, that he had sent him to Rohtas to meet Mirza Kamran, with another body of Afghans. It has been rightly said by Dr. Qanungo that if Sher Shah had discovered military talents in Todarmal Khatri of Lahore and entrusted him with the arduous task of getting the fort of Rohtas constructed in the hostile Gakkar territory; his son "made a more conspiouous discovery of Hemu, who became the pillar of fortune of the disintegrating Sur regime after the death of Islam Shah."

Islam Shah followed the policy of employing Hindu officials and clerks in the civil administration. Badaoni has mentioned that they enjoyed prosperity, as they had a comparatively easier and lucrative jobs, which according to some contemporaries was due to their capacity of extorting taxes or even embezzling of revenues.

The Afghan nobles feared Islam Shah, as he was ruthless and had ordered public execution of Khawas Khan, removal of Jalal bin Jalu, Qutb Khan *Zaid* and other prominent Afghans. He is also reported to have taken thirteen other nobles to the fort of Gwalior as prisoner. In order to maintain his power he began to rely on Hemu more and more. Although this enraged the old Afghan nobility he promoted six thousand *sawars* to the position of an officer and thereafter *Amir*. Islam Shah ruled with an iron hand

and during eight years broke the backbone of the Afghan nobility, so assiduously built by Sher Shah.[17]

In short, beneath the stormy surface of Islam Shah's reign, all was quiet and progress, peace and prosperity prevailed. The reforms introduced by Sher Shah, the administrative measures initiated by him, were allowed to attain fruition. Roads, serais continued to be built and maintained. Historians have praised Sher Shah, although he reigned only for five years, but his son's achievements have been ignored, despite his over eight years rule.

Islam Shah not only allowed more and more powers to Hemu, but also granted respite to Hindu Rajas of Marwar, Rewa, Mewar, Bundelkhand and the Siwaliks. They became active again. In Mewat Haji Khan Batain, the fauzdar and a close associate as well as ally of Hemu rose to power. His services were utilised in Marwar, in place of Khawas Khan. Consequently Islam Shah's authority began to be recognised in Mewar, as of Kumbhalmir in Marwar. According to the chronogram of Sher Tahir Deccan, when Islam Shah and Mahmood King of Gujarat, as well as Nizam Ulmulk Babir, were sovereign Prince in the Deccan in 961 A.H. Islam Shah was the Sultan of Delhi, "under whom Hindustan flourished like a rose-garden."

Islam Shah's death

During the last years of his reign Islam Shah had to face the danger of Humayun's renewed attempt to regain India, the hostility of Afghan rebels, and his own physical ailments. Badaoni had gone to the extreme of recording that when Islam Shah heard of Humayun, having crossed the *Nilab*, he mobilised and moved out of Delhi to fight. Mirza Kamran who was a fugitive from Humayun, was treated with coldness. Although he had deputed Hemu to escort him, but he soon retreated to Gwalior for pleasure and treatment. He left Punjab to Hemu. In the words of Badaoni, "Among the forces which overthrew him was,it is said a carbuncle which appeared in the neighbourhood of his seat, others assert it was cancer."[18]

Although narratives differ about Islam Shah's serious illness and his reactions to Humayun's, march to Delhi, but all agree that he had retired to Gwalior. Naturally he left the important charge of Lahore to his brother-in-law, Ahmad Khan Sur, and Delhi to Hemu. The charge of the Sarkar of Sambhal was entrusted to Mubariz Khan, his own cousin and brother-in-law. He was also given a command of 20,000 troops.

Consequently when Islam Shah breathed his last at Gwalior on 30 October 1553, after eight year's rule, his son, who was hardly six years old (according to Badaoni twelve years old) was in the field to be proclaimed as his successor.[19]

But Mubariz Khan, who had been raised to high command by Islam Shah, with the hope that he would act as the regent of his infant son Firuz, betrayed the trust and murdered the infant heir to the throne. A gruesome account of the heinous crime has been penned down in the *Makhzan-i-Afghana* thus :

"But, after three days, Mubariz Khan, a son of Mian Nizam, Sher Shah's who had his sister, Bibi Bai by name, in marriage and was so high in favour with him that he did not change his apartment without his consent and was delighted in his company, entered Sher Shah's private apartments, under pretence of seeing his sister, and assassinated Firuz Khan, inspite of all the entreaties and lamentatious of his mother, Bibi Bai, who said, 'Pray, do not kill my son: I consider him my only eyelight; and will take an oath, that I will resign all claims to royalty, and with my son, depart for the Deccan.'"

According to Al-Badaoni, Bibi Bai, fell on the feet of Mubariz Khan and besought him piteously saying--"Ah! my brother, spare the life of this poor harmless boy, and let me take my own way and bear him away to some place, where no one will have a trace of him, and when he will have nothing to do with sovereignty nay, will not mention the name of kingship.'[20]

But the pitiless tyrant did not pay any heed to Bibi Bai's lamentations, and entering the palace cut off the boy's head under the very eyes of his mother. Islam Shah was apprehensive of Mubariz Khan's intentions and he had warned his wife to keep clear of his brother if she wanted to save her child's life. Bibi Bai only exclaimed that her brother spent all his time in amusing himself, and the role of royalty was in no way suitable for him. According to Badaoni too Mubariz Khan was accustomed "to the profession of music and dancing." He was known to be one of the best musicians of his time. He was weak and incompetent and given to a life of ease. He used to be called "Adli" — a name which they perverted to "Andhali" — which had the commonly accepted significance of "Blind" — literally a *blind woman*. He was commonly called Adeli — the FOOLISH. The nickname was given to him because he spent his life in pleasure, amusement and musical entertainment.[21]

As Sultan

Having murdered the rightful heir to the throne Mubariz khan ascended the throne on November 2, 1553 A.D. He started to appease the nobles by lavishly distributing wealth and titles. According to Al-Badaoni he tried to imitate the Tughlqe Shah, who used to throw arrows tipped with gold and whatever poor person's house, they fell, they were bestowed that amount in money and the Sultan used to take back the *Katila-bash*. However such a practice could not last long.

According to Neamutullah also, Mubariz Khan opened the door of his treasuries, and loaded the people with bounties, Five hundred tankas were paid for bringing back the arrows back. He was hopeless, inefficient and squandered the treasure. In the words of Dr. Ishwari Prasad, Mubariz was "hopelessly debauched and entirely indifferent to public affairs, he was the last man in the world to save the Afghan empire from falling into the ruin which threatened that."

In order to run the administration, Mubariz Khan, first made Shamsher Khan (Shams Khan), a slave, and a younger brother of Khawas Khan as well as Daulat Khan Lohari as his Vizier. The incumbent was a "new — Muslim", a protege of the Lohari factions.

Adil Shah and Hemu.

Unable to face the anger of the Afghan nobles Adil Shah, who was the son of Nizam Shah, the younger brother of Sher Shah, was at tenterhooks. He gave "uncontrolled authority to Hemu, whom Islam Shah had gradually elevated from the position of the police superintendent of the bazars and confirmer of punishments, and had by degrees made into a trusted confident. He now gave him the superintendence of all important affairs both military and civil."[22]

According to Neamutullah also, Hemu hailing from Rewari and a surveyor of the kitchen, "was raised to high dignity, and gradually admitted to intimacy with Sultan Adil, or rather Adeli (the Foolish)," In comparison to it, the version of Al-Badaoni seems to be more plausible. Hemu had already been elevated to the rank of trusted minister and Islam Shah had also recognised his military talent. Adil Shah, having committed the heinous crime of murdering the rightful claimant to the throne, had no option, but to elevate Hemu to the rank of Prime Minister and controller of military affairs. As he had already antagonised his kinsmen, he hastely summoned a durbar in the fort of Gwalior.

As soon as the news of Adil Shah's accession reached the Afghan nobles in the various provinces, each of them, in his own place, actuated by the desire after the throne, turned his view to rebellion; and from country to country, from town to town, all was put in a state of sedition.[23] The greater part of the Afghan nobility fled away and there was a general dispersal of them from Delhi and Agra. Adil Shah's authority rapidly declined. In the words of Neamutullah, "...power, and a numerous attendance, that are the pre-requisites of royalty, had totally disappeared and the ground officers of the army all fled, from mutual distrust."

The governing Council of the Sultan was in a precarious state. No one respected or dreaded Adil Shah. When the council or durbar met at Gwalior, all nobles who were present there, spoke of unheard of things and behaved in a manner without precedent. Everybody thought it wiser to retire to private life, that was the safest way to escape any catastrophe. In the words of Abul Fazl, Hemu rose to high rank, "and became the prime minister of that tyrant, who spent all his time in sport and amusement and bodily lusts, and neglected affairs."[24]

Murder of Sermust Khan.

Sultan Adil Shah in Council decided to dispossess Shah Mohammd Fermuli of his estate in Kanauj and transferred them to Sermust Khan Serbunni.[25] This enraged Shah Muhammad's young and bold son Sekundar Khan and he started using abusive language in the Council. Shah Muhammad was sick at that time. However Sermust Khan, who was a tall and robust man, challenged Sekundar Khan, who drew his sword and killed him on the spot. Having became desperate, he began attacking all those who opposed him. Some of the Afghan chiefs were killed on the spot. Thus within a few months after the death of Islam Shah, rebellion was widespread in the country.

Adil was aghast at seeing the incident. A general uproar and tumult followed and all present rushed to apprehend Sikandar. But the latter was so brave that with the sword in his hand, he cut down or wounded most of them who turned towards him. Even the Sultan, apprehending danger to his self, ran to his private apartment, and bolted the door. Thus Sikandar could do no harm to him.[26]

But the riotous scenes in the durbar were a sign of the weakness of the government and an open invitation to anarchy.

Sikundar Killed : While most of the nobles had fled, Adli's own brother-in-law, Ibrahim Khan Sur, attacked Sikundar and killed him. Shah muhammad Fermulli was despatched by Daulat khan Lohani. Although he had been previously warned by Taj Kerrani, a brother of Suleman, but he did not heed that, in consequence was killed in the riotouss council.

Taj Kerrani seeking the condition decided to flee towards Bengal. Sultan Adil Shah scenting danger, wanted to pursue him in person. At this time Hemu offered to do the job if some elephants were placed under his command. So he was charged with the pursuit by Adil Shah. Hemu overtook "the highly insolent grandee of Islam Shah and the captor of Khawas Khan at Chibramow, about forty miles from Agra and thirty from Kanauj."[27] Though defeated by Hemu, he managed to effect his escape to Chunar. Thus began Hemu's conquests against the rebellious Afghans. He crossed the river with only one hundred elephants engaged the Afghan rebels and routed them. Taj Khan fled to Bengal.

Notes and References

1. *Akbarnama*, Vol. I. pp. 615-619. Dictionary meaning of a huckster, is a retailer of small wares a hawker a pedler. Hemu was neither of them. He came from a respectable family of Dhusar Bhargavas of Rewari.
2. *Mantakhabu-T-Tawarikh,* Vol. I. p. 902 : cf. *Akbarnama* Vol. I. pp. 351-359. On the other hand *Tarikh-i-Sher Shahi* mentions Salim Khan only as Jalal Khan and Islam Khan.
3. *Sher Shah and His Times.,* p. 413. fn. 2. Abul Fazl has mentioned that as the Sarkar of the Subah of Agra and also records the existence of a stone fort there, built by Sher Shah.
4. *Tarikh-i-Sher Shahi,* trs. E.C. Bayley. 3rd ed. 1957. p. 137.
5. Ibid. p. 139.
6. *Sher Shah and His Times;* pp. 438-439; cf. Neamatullah, *The Makhzan,* trs. Dorn., p. 142-150.
7. Neamutullah : p. 146.
8. Ibid : p. 147 : also *The Successors of Sher Shah,* by Nirod Bhushan Roy, (1934) pp. 9-10.
9. Neamutullah. pp. 150-152.
10. Ibid. pp. 153-154. cf. *The Successors of Sher Shah;* pp. 10-12.
11. *Sher Shah and His Times.,* p. 439 According to Dr. Qanungo Adil Khan fled towards Bundelkhand by way of Chandwar and was not heard of any more.

12. Ibid., pp. 440-441; Mankot is situated at a distance of five or six *Krohs* from Bin-Bin and has been identified by Raverty as being 19 miles north-east of Sialkot and eight miles south-west of Jammu. It is on the east bank of the Chenab.
13. Ibid., p. 448 cf. Badaoni, text, i. p. 381.
14. *The Successors of Sher Shah.*, p. 89.
15. Ibid., 40.
16. Railway Station in Madhya Pradesh.
17. *Waqiat-Mushtaqi,* quoted by Iqtidar Hussain Siddiqi in his book — *Some Aspects of Afghan Despotism* in India; also Neamutullah, p. 170.
18. *Muntakhabu-T-Tawarikh,* Vol. I. pp. 530-531; also cf. The Successors of Sher Shah, pp. 42-43.
19. *Muntakhabu-T-Tawarikh* has recorded the date of Islam Shah's death as 22 November 1554 A.D. (961 A.H.) i.e. after a rule of nine years and six months; and T.N. Chaudhari has mentioned the same in *The Mughal Empire,* (Bhavan Series) Vol. VII p. 92. But according to all other reliable sources Islam Shah had expired on 30 October 1553 A.D.
20. Ibid., p. 535 : also cf. Neamatullah, pp. 170-171.
21. Ibid. p. 171.
22. *Muntakhabu-T-Tawarikh* Vol. I. p. 537; also *The Successors of Sher Shah* pp. 65-66.
23. Neamutullah., p. 172.
24. *Akbarnama,* Vol. I. pp. 655-657.
25. Ferishta : trs. Eng. Vol. I. P. 146. According to Neamutullah Surmust Khan was "seller of stones", p. 172.
26. Ibid : cf. *The Makhzan-i-Afghana* also p. 173.
27. District Faruckhabad, U.P. Chhibramau, tahsil head-quarters, the town on the grand trunk road and so prepared. It possesses he ruins of a large castle and of an old *sarai* : *The Successors of Sher* Shah, p. 67.

CHAPTER-IV

Conquests of Hemu

According to Abul Fazl Hemu fought twenty-two battles and won all of them, for his master.[1] But as the complete details. the names of places and the adversaries defeated have not been specified, no one has attempted to list them and thus bring out the non-pareil achievements of the remarkable general, who knew no defeat.

According to available sources the riotous scenes at the Gwalior durbar resulted in the murder of Surmust khan, the consequent killing of Sikundar and the flight of Taj Karrani to Bengal. These events threw the entire Afghan kingdom, left by Islam Shah, into firment, and the Afghan nobles rose in revolt openly[2].

Adil Shah did succeed in murdering the infant heir to the throne, but in due course as many as three contenders emerged in the field in and around Agra-Delhi viz. Salim Khan Sur, Sikundar Sur and Ibrahim Sur. Besides them there were two other contenders in the Eastern Provinces, Ibrahim Khan and Muhammad Khan Sur or Shamsuddin Muhammad Shah Ghazi.

Revolt of Salim Khan Sur.

According to Abul Fazl, Adil Shah was the son of Nizam Khan, the younger brother of Sher Shah. He has one son and three daughters, and a strange thing that happened, was that when the son became the ruler, the husbands of the three daughters rose to high rank. They were Salim Khan Sur, Sikundar Sur and Ibrahim Sur.

Salim Khan Sur was the first to raise the banner of revolt, but that was easily suppressed by Hemu. That was the first achievement of Hemu and Adli was very much impressed by his military prowess.

Battle of Ajmer: Subedar Junaid Khan of Ajmer, along with his general Daulat Khan revolted and were challenged by Hemu's army. Both of them were defeated in battles fought in the vicinity of Ajmer. These second and the third victories of Hemu were still more unexpected and may be termed as the first three of the twenty-two battles won by him for his master Adil Shah.

Firmulli's abortive revolt: The trouble started when Adil Shah tried to redistribute estates in a common council, which was attended by all the nobles (Omras). Dispossession of Shah Mohamed Fermulli of his estates in Kannauj, and it transfer to Sermust Khan was resented by Fermulli's hot headed son. Sikender Khan exclaimed, "to what degree have things come, that the estates are ate taken from us, and settled on *a seller of stones*." Shah Mahomed tried to calm down his son but Sikender Khan was furious and ran amuck in the council hall.

Sermust Khan, who equally a tall and robust man, seized Sikender's garment, as though to pacify him; but in fact, with the intention to secure him in this way; and said :"My dear what is the reason of such anger and exasperation." immediately following that Surmust Khan seized Sikender Khan by throat, but the young opponent was quicker in stabbing him to death. Adil Shah was attacked and he fled to the inner apartments, and was saved by by Ibrahim Khan Sur. Surmust Khan was attacked and Muhammad Khan Firmulli was put to death by Daulat Khan Lohani.[4]

Taj Karrani's flight: Another important Afghan noble, who had scented danger to Muhammad Khan Fermulli, and had cautioned him earlier at the gates of citadel of Gwalior, stayed outside the audience-hall. According to *the Makhzan*, he "explained to him the precarious state of the council : and told him, that affairs had taken such a turn, that no one further respected or dreaded Adli, all present having spoken unheard of things in the very council, and behaved in a manner without precedent; it was therefore the safest way not to frequent the council anymore."

Thus Taj Karrani invited Fermulli to join him, and repair to a place affording security against misery, there to spend the rest of their life in mutual friendship. Fermulli rejected the offer and thus lost his life.

Taj Karrani went to his house and made all preparations for flight to Bengal. Taking all his dependents he "took the route of Bengal."[5] He was allowed to flee unmolested.

Battle of Chibramau : As soon as Sultan Adil Shah learnt of Taj Karrani's departure, he decided to pursue him in person. But Hemu offered to do the job for him, by dealing effectively with the fugitive. Adli charged him with the pursuit. Hemu overtook the "highly insolent grandee of Islam Shah and the captor, of Khawas Khan" at Chibramau. After having been engaged near Kanauj and defeated, he fled to Chunar.[6]

Adli committed a fatal blunder in hastily returning to Gwalior, after the battle of Chibramau. He did not bother to pursue Taj Khan, the work was left to Hemu, who grabbed the opportunity. Adli showed his lack of vigour and absence of martial spirit.

Taj Khan was soon joined by his brothers Imad, Sulaiman and Khwaja Ilyas, the governor of Khawaspur Tanda as well as certain other parganas on the banks of the Ganges. According to Ferishta, "In his progress (he) seized the public money and other effects belonging to his brothers and others of his tribe, who held lands in the province of Khawaspur Tanda."[7] On hearing that Adli was compelled to join Hemu at Chunar, wherein, "The two forces confronted each other across a river until Hemu, by a sudden dash gained the other bank with a few elephants and routed the rebels after a desperate struggle".[8] Capture of Chunar enhanced the prestige of Hemu and no wonder that he was thereafter hailed as Vikramaditya.

The Chunar fort in ancient times is said to have been a place of retirement of Bhartinatha, the younger brother of the famous Vikramaditya of Ujjainani, who had turned a *yogi*, doing penance on the rock of Chunar, on the bank of Ganges.[9] The temple of

Bhartinatha exists even today. During medieval India it came into great prominence, as Sher Shah obtained its possession by marrying the daughter of a local chieftain and acquiring immense treasure. Abbas Sarwani has given minutest details, about the transfer of Chunar fort to Sher Shah by Lad Malika, as childless widow of Taj Khan Sarang Khani, the commandant of the same, who held the fort for the Mughal emperor after 1528 A.D. Prior to that Sultan Ibrahim Lodi had entrusted to Taj Khan Sarang Khani the prestigious fort along with the royal treasures.

According to Neamutullah six hundred mans of pure gold, besides many other rarities, and much of the tresures of the kingdom had been handed over to Sher Shah. Besides that Sher Shah got-possession of the pergannas near the fort and strengthened his resources still further by inheriting sixty *mans* of gold from Guhar Kusain widow of Nasir Khan. Lad Malika had already given Sher Shah a present "consisting of 150 of the most exceedingly valuable jewels, and *seven* mans of pearls, and 150 *mans* of gold, and many other articles and ornaments."[10]

It will be evident from the above that capture of the fort of Chunar was strategically important and valuable from the treasures kept therein. Due to incessant warfare. two things were uppermost to keep the army, cavalry and war-elephants, in fighting trim, viz. availability of food, and money for the soldiers. Hemu ensured supply of both the items, so that the rank and file of Rajputs and Afghans, flocked to his banner.

Neighbourhood pergunnas : Taj Kerrani in his fight against Hemu and Adli was aided by Sulaiman Imad and Khwaja Ilyas, who controlled the pergunnas on the banks of Ganges in the vicinity of Chunar. As they were anxious to fight Adli so Hemu engaged them and brought all of them to the knees."[11]

In token of the service rendered by Hemu on this occasion and the honour gained by his extraordinary valour as well as military prowess, Adli bestowed upon him the title of Vikramaditya. Abul Fazl also corroborates it by mentioning that Hemu prior to the battles of Delhi and Panipat had assumed this title, "for sometime past "[12] According to him he preserved the nominal sovereignty for Adli and waged great wars against his opponents. He applied great names to himself.

Al-Badaoni on the other hand records that Hemu assumed this title after the capture of Delhi in October 1556.[13] Nizamuddin says Hemu blew the trumpet of his pride in Delhi and himself assumed the title of Raja Vikramjit.

On the basis of Al-Badaoni, Professor Satish Chandra has also mentioned in his article on Hemu, his ancestary and place in history, that "After the conquest of Delhi Hemu had been given the title of Vikramjit."

But it has not been clarified by whom? There was no trace of Adli near about Delhi or Agra in 1555-1556. According to Abul Fazl he was busy revelling in the fort of Chunar.[14] Moreover such titles are usually awarded and not assumed. So assumption and award of this title after victories in the East of Chunar is more plausible.

It is evident from the details available that battles in and round Chunar, and its neighbouring pergunnas, against Taj Karrani, Sulaiman Imad, and Khawaja Ilyas were fought collectively as well as severally. All of these three battles appear to have been fought on the banks of Ganges and were won by Hemu. The opponents were defeated decisively. Along with Taj Karrani, Rukn Khan Nuhani was also engaged and "was made to tread the land of annihilation."[15]

Battle of Charkata : After victories against supporter of Taj Karrani, Hemu had to fight a battle against Kodian, near Charkata, and he won that too."[16]

Attack on Bengal : Taj Karrani, although defeated had not surrendered. He fled to Jaunpur and joined his brother Ahmad Khan. Both of then decided to march towards the East. Hemu entreated his master Adli to remain at Chunar, and allow him to deal with the Karranis. The permission was gladly accorded and Hemu, with his Afghan army and war-like elephants pursued the Karranis right upto the borders of Bengal. Taj Karrani had taken shelter with his brother, near about Khawaspur Tanda, where he held some jagirs.[17]

Khawaspur-Tanda lay on the frontier of Muhammad Khan Sur's jagir, and was identical with the pergana Mohaniya, which lay south-west of Sahasram. According to the findings of Dr. Qanungo, Chayanpur in the pergana became a favourite residence of some branches of Sher Shah's family. It contained the tomb of Athyar Khan, who married a daughter of Sher Shah, besides many Pathan tombs of their family. Sahasram was the home and headquarters of Mian Hasan, and it was here that Sher Shah built his mausolem. About twenty miles miles due south lies the mighty fort of Rohtas. So its conquest was equally important and made Hemu a non-pareil general of his times.

From Ajmer in Rajasthan to Khawaspur-Tanda in the East, can be termed to be the first round of Hemu's battles and the resultant conquests of territories for his master Adil Shah Sur, In this round Hemu fought as many as nine battles, which earned for him name and fame. The time taken to achieve them, could not have been more than a year, i.e. 1553-1554 A.D.

Adil Shah had ascended the throne only in October-November 1553 after the death of Islam Shah and the gruesome murder of the infant heir, Firuz. Consequently he was challenged throughout the length and breadth of North India soon after. As the Afghan nobles were sore and non-cooperative, Hemu came to the rescue of Adil Shah, who resided mostly at Gwalior. In all probability Hemu being at the helm of civil and military administration at Delhi, was forced to take up cudgels on Adli's behalf. With what rapidity he met the adversaries is a marvel. To traverse the distance from Ajmer in the West to Khwaspur-Tanda in the East, must have taken at least six months or even more. To be in saddle or on elephant howdah, most of the time was a remarkable feat, and management of the army towards victory in as many as nine battles great achievement.

IInd round of battles : Although Adil and Hemu succeeded in pursuing and defeating Taj Karrani and establishing his sway in the East, the Afghan nobles in and around Gwalior, Kalpi and Bayana became estranged. Persecution of persons of eminence like Daulat Khan Jilwani and Firoz Khan Kakar, who had been loyal to Adli alienated other Afghan noblemen.[18]

Due to dogged fight in the East Hemu and Adli took the risk of inviting rival contenders to the throne at Delhi and Agra. Adli was already suspicious and jealous of Ibrahim Khan Sur, who emerged as a formidable contender to the throne. Adli is reported to have issued secret orders for his arrest, but his wife, Adli's own sister, hearing of his brother's design, acquainted Ibrahim, her husband of the danger. Ibrahim fled from Chunar, and took the route to Bayana, where his father Ghazi Khan was the governor of Hindown. According to Abul Fazl, "Battles took place between Hemu and Ibrahim, who was a claimant for the Sultanate and the former was always victorious." Adil despatched Isa Khan Niazi after him and they fought a battle in the vicinity of Kalpi. Ibrahim gained the day initially.[19]

Emboldened by his initial success, Ibrahim Khan Sur made a bid to capture, Gwalior, Delhi and Agra. Adli on learning about that, hastened to suppress the possible usurpation, and disengaged himself from Karranis in the East. When he reached the river Jon, Ibrahim Khan made overtures and sent message saying —"If Rai Hussain Jilawain and Bihar Khan Sarwain, to whom Islam Shah gave the title of Azam Humayun, with some others of the Amirs noble and renowned, come and reassure me, then will I in reliance upon their assurances agree to make submission to you."[20]

According to Ferishta, instead of opposing Ibrahim Khan Sur outright, Adli began to negotiate,

"promising that, if the king would send Hoossein Khan and other chief with assurances he would submit. The king complied with the request, by promises, and by address, to espouse his cause. Mahomed Shah Adli finding himself betrayed fled to Chunar and contended himself with the government of the Eastern provinces, while Ibrahim Khan retained possession of the Western territory."[21]

For the time being Ibrahim, having seized the throne rallied round him a number of Afghan nobles and got the *Khutba* read in his name. He took the title of Sultan Mohamad and became powerful at Agra. But he could not enjoy sovereignty for a while, as his authority was challenged by Ahmed Shah, husband of his younger sister and a cousin of Adil Shah. He was nephew of the late Sher Shah, whose sister was married to Adli. He declared open war against Adli, and assuming the title of Sultan Sikundar, proceeded towards Delhi and Agra. He was anxious to regain Bayana, his father's jagir.

In the words of Ferishta, "Ahmad Khan, having procured the aid of Heibut Khan, and other chiefs, who had been created and nobles by the late Salim Shah, assumed the title of Sikundar Shah, and marching with 10,000 or 12,000 horse towards Agra, encamped at Kurra (Kaggaraul?) within 20 miles of that city. Ibrahim Khan opposed him with 70,000 horse, and some notion of the splendour of his train may be formed when it is stated that no less that two hundred officers occupied tents lines with velvet, each having the privilege of beating the *nobut*."[22]

Battle of Farrah : Soon after Ibrahim Khan had captured the throne of Delhi, Sultan Sikandar gathered motley army of then thousand men from Punjab and wanted to seize Delhi and Agra. The two contesting armies of Ibrahim Khan and Ahmad Khan, met each other at Farrah, a village 10 *Kos* North-East from Agra.[23] Sikundur Shah considering his force too small to oppose the formidable army of Ibrahim Khan, sent a message to him, offering him terms of peace. A treaty was proposed, by which the whole of the country from Delhi to Eastern extremity of Hind was to belong to Ibrahim, and Sikundar was to content himself with the Punjab and Multan. It was also agreed that if the vast treasure of Adli fell in the hands of Ibrahim, both of them will share the same.

But Ibrahim Khan, according to Ferishta and Neamutullah, got puffed up with his shortlived success, and refused to listen to the terms offered. He thought that by giving consent to the terms, his Afghan supporters would regard that as his weakness, so action was postponed but it could not be long delayed.[24]

Consequently engagements between the two contenders continued and Ibrahim Khan suffered a setback. When Sikundur gained an upperhand, Ibrahim Khan fled to Sambhal. He had already become oblivious of the challenge he was to face from Adli. Sikender Khan was obliged to repair to Punjab, so as to oppose Humayun, who was hectically making preparation to recover his lost territories in India. In Sirhind he eventually fought a battle but was defeated.[25]

First Battle of Kalpi : As soon as Ibrahim reached Kalpi from Sambhal, Hemu's army challenged him. After suffering a defeat at Kalpi Ibrahim fled to Bayana, to seek shelter with his father at Bayana. Hemu pursued him and besieged Bayana. He had with him "certain eminent amirs, and five hundred elephants like storm clouds (for blackness), and unlimited treasure to proceed towards agra and Delhi."[26]

Second battle of Kalpi : Ibrahim had come to Kalpi after having collected a fresh army, took up a strong position, and showed a resolute determination, to with-stand Hemu. "such as perhaps Rustam, if anyone, displayed before." In Badaoni's words. "but for all that, by the decree of Almighty, he was not successful. Although he had praiseworthy qualities belonging to Kings, he fought sixteen or seventeen battles, and on every occasion after gaining a success met with a defeat". Hemu regarding Ibrahim "as his own special prey, considered it essential to overthrow him."[27]

Battle of Khanwah, and *Siege of Bayana*

Ibrahim Khan after his defeat at Kalpi, fled towards Bayana with all speed, and Hemu pursuing him arrived there with equal alacrity. After taking a body of Nuhani and Afghan cultivators and land holders of Bayana again, Ibrahim readied himself to meet Hemu. Making a right attack on him the following morning, he fought a fierce battle near to the township of *Khanwah*, ten *Krohs* distant from Bayana, but Hemu rolled him and inflicted a defeat upon him, so that he was compelled to fortify himself in the fortress of Bayana. Hemu attacked the fort every day, subjecting that to heavy bombardment. Hemu kept up the siege of the fort for three months, despite the raging famine in and around Agra, Bayana and Delhi. Ghazi Khan, the father of Ibrahim Khan kept the fort of Bayana, provided with the supplies by way of the mountain passes to the westwards of Bayana.

According to Al-Badaoni '...when blockaded the fortress of Bayana — God's people (?) were crying for bread and taking each other's lives, a hundred thousand sacred lives were as thought for a single grain of barley whereas the elephants of Hemu's army, which numbered five hundred, were fed solely upon RICE, and OIL and SUGAR..."[28]

Battle of Agra — 1554 A.D. (962 A.H.) In the meantime Hemu received an urgent message from Adli that Muhammad Khan Sur, had assumed the title of Sultan Jalalu-d-Din, and was marching with an army like ants and locusts. He must have made way for Jaunpur and thence for Kalpi and Agra. Adli rightly felt alarmed and frantically sent message to Hemu in these words, " At all costs come to me at once as I am confronted by a powerful enemy". Hemu was thus forced to abandon the siege of Bayana and as soon as he crossed Mandagar (Mandakar — Mandagarh) six *krohs* from Agra, he was attacked by Ibrahim, but Hemu defeated him once again. Ibrahim fled towards Alwar.[29]

Battle of Alwar : Ibrahim after obtaining reinforcements from Haji Khan Alwari again set about to accomplish his own objects. But he was confronted by Hemu's nephew Mahipal (wrongly spelled as Tharpal) with a fully equipped army. This engagement took place before his flight to Bhatta and Punna. Haji Khan was not pleased at Ibrahim's coming, nor he sent any assistance to him. The narratives about that are conflicting. But as Haji Khan Alwari (Mewati)'s relations with Hemu and Mahipal were cordial, he was not expected to oppose Hemu's army.[30]

According to some Haji Khan set his face against Ibrahim, because of his successive reverses and ultimate flight towards Orissa.

Battle of Chupurgatta (1555 A.D.): According to Al-Badaoni "Adli and Muhammad Khan Gauria were at that time sitting down over against one another, with the river Jamuna between them, at a place called Chappar Khatta fifteen *Krohs* from Kalpi." But Ferishta has given more details. According the him, Hemu had joined Adli at Chunar and then proceeded against Muhammad Shah Sur of Bengal, "who, avoiding him by crossing the hills near Rohtas, entered the country of Bundelkhand, whither being pursued by Hemu, the two armies came to action at the village of Chupurgatta, thirty miles from Kalpi and Muhammad Shah Sur of Bengal was slain.[31]

Hemu had swooped suddenly down upon the army of Bengal. The surprise was so complete that they were seized with panic coupled with confusion and fled away. After this victory and the slaying of Muhammad Shah, Adli appointed Shahabaz Khan Governor of Bengal and returned to Chunar.

Al-Badaoni has also given a graphic description of the battle of Chupurghatta in these words," Gauria confidently relying upon his superior force to overcome the force of Adli, had drawn up his cavalry and infantry and elephants to a number surpassing all computation and was every moment expecting victory, when suddenly the scale turned against him, *and Hemu swept down upon him like a comet*, and no sooner did he reach the ranks of the picked elephants after crossing the river Jamuna, then he swooped down upon the army of Gauria, taking them unawares as does the army of sleep, and making the night-assault gave no one time so much as to lift his hand."[32]

There was utter confusion after the battle, no one knew his head from his heels, nor his turban from his shoes. Most of the amirs were slain, and the rest took to flight. In the words of Al-Badaoni,"...after this heaven-given victory and unforeseen triumph," Adli proceeded to Chunar and appointed Hemu, who was already the commander-in-chief of his army, to combat the Mughals who were planning to reoccupy Delhi and Agra.

Ibrahim lived in Orissa under the shelter of the Raja of Jagannath, but during this inter regnum he hatched a plan to conquer Bengal, but fell a victim to the treachery of Sulaiman Karrani of Bengal and was assassinated in 1567 A.D. According to Nirod Bhushan Roy, Ibrahim was a notable figure of the Sur dynasty. In his words, "Graceful in appearance, possessed of refinement, he was a typical knight-errant who delighted in war. Fighting more than a dozen losing battles in the short space of two years (1554-5), he yet did not lose faith in his star."[33]

Thus ended the two claimants to the throne of Delhi, Salim Khan Sur and Sultan Ibrahim. Bengal too became devoid of a powerful ruler; so from Ajmer to Bayana, Delhi to Kalpi-Chunar — Khawaspur Tanda extending to Bengal the writ of Adli and Hemu prevailed. They had a powerful army, fully equipped with horses and elephants, and immense treasure at their disposal.

Plight of Sikandar Shah : Having received news about the warring factions between the Afghan nobles, Humayun started on his reconquest of India in November 1554. Sikandar's general Tatar Khan Kashi, who was incharge of the fortress of Rohtas, evacuated that. Humayun retook the city of Lahore on February 24, 1555, without any resistance. The road was clear to Delhi, and the Mughals defeated Shahabaz Khan at Dipalpur (Montogomery district of Punjab in Pakistan). The Mughals reached Jalandhar and then a battle took place at Machiwara. The Afghans were defeated. Sikandar personally took the field with a numerous army, comprising of cavalry, infantry, elephants and also a park of artillery. Furious battle took place at Sirhind. The Mughal general Tardi Beg Khan defeated Sikandar's army and his brothers including Kalapahar were slain by 22 June 1555. Sikander made a desparate attempt and hurled his army against the Mughal army's wing led by Bairam Khan, Tardi Beg Khan and Shah Abul-l-Maoli. The Afghans were surrounded and routed badly. Sikandar was compelled to flee and take shelter in the Siwalik hills of Punjab. Sikandar, the third formidable candidate for the throne of Delhi, was out of the arena for the time-being.

Hemu was the only general left to face the advancing hordes of the Mughals under able general and Humayun. Ibrahim had already been ousted from Delhi and Agra. The entire country was in a disunited and chaotic state, disaffected to the Afghan rulers. There was famine and due to incessant wars, between the different rivals to the throne, there was anarchy alround. At this propitious hour, Humayun regained the throne of Delhi. The lost throne was at last occupied, but was still insecure.

Anarchy and Famine : 1555 A.D. In the words of Nirod Bhushan, "The violence and rapacity of the predatory chiefs combined with the marching and counter-marching of troops across the country produced their natural consequences."[34]

The situation was aggravated due to insufficient rainfall in that year. Due to violence and anarchy, the fields could not be tilled, so food stuffs became very scarce. Hunger and famine stalked the countryside. Grains became very dear. One seer of Jawar grain sold at a rupee, and people are reported to have lived on wild herbs and roofs. Disease spread in the area. Badaoni speaks vigorously about the unspeakable misery, which occured in the heartland of India. To sum up the year 1554-5 A.D. (962 A.H.) was an eventful year in Indian history. The battles of Farah, Machiwara, Sirhind, Kalpi, Khanwah, Chuppurghatta-were all fought with success by the Afghans under Hemu, Sikandar Shah Sur was discomfited in the brief space of only twelve months. Ibrahim had already disappeared from the scene, Sikandar retreated to the hills of Punjab, while Muhammad Shah had died. There remained only two powerful contenders for the throne, viz. Humayun and Hemu, Adli's general and prime minister.

Notes and References

1. *Akbarnama*, Vol. II., p.45.
2. *The Makhzan*, pp. 172-173; also *The Successors of Sher Shah*; x p.65.
4. Neamutullah : pp. 172-173
5. Ibid. p.173. also Tripathi, Dr.R.P., *Mughal Empire* : p.158
6. Chunar on Charanadrigadha — twenty miles east of Mirzapur, U.P. is celebrated for its old and strong hill fort on the banks of the river Ganges.
7. *History of the Rise of Mahomedan Power in India*, Vol. II(trs. Briggs)., p.146
8. Prasad,, Dr. Ishwari; Humayun, p.194
9. *Archaeological Survey of India*, Vol. II. Monumental antiquities and Inscriptions, .N.W.P. and Oudh, 1897.
10. *Tarikh-i-Sher Shahi*, pp. 55-59 : Ahmad Yadgar give a different enumeration, but gives the total value at nine lacs of rupees.
11. *Akbar-Nama*, Vol. II. p.45.
12. Ibid; also p.50.

13. *Muntakhabu-T-Tawarikh,* Vol. II. p. 7; also *The Successors of Sher Shah.,* pp.90-91 and the footnotes on.91.
14. *Akbarnama* : Vol. II. p.46.
15. Ibid., p.45.
16. Dr. Manhar Gopal's article. Perhaps the place was Rankatta near Hilalahed, six Kos N.W. form Agra.
17. *Sher Shah and His Times.,* pp.44-54., fn.1. also *Martiner's Eastern India,* ii, pp.455 and 460; as well as i; 560
18. Ferishta., (Briggs) Vol. II. pp.146-147.
19. *Muntakhabu-T-Tawarikh,* Vol., pp.541-542.
20. Ibid.
21. *Rise of Mahomedan Power in India,* Vol. II.pp.146-147.
22. Ibid. Vol. II. p.147; *nobut* Musical band — composed of nine instruments, confined to Kings, but conferred by them on governors, to be used only in their governments and in the absence of the royal family.
23. *Muntakhabu-T-Tawarikh,* Vol. I. p.542.
24. Ferishta : (Briggs); Vol. II., p.147 also cf.
    Dr. Ishwari Prasad, *Humayun.* p.196
25. *Muntakhabu-T-Tawarikh,* Vol. I. pp.547-548.
26. Ibid.
27. Ibid : p.548.
28. Ibid., Vol. I. pp.550-551.
29. Ibid., Vol. I. pp. 552--553. Cf. Ferishta, according to whom Ibrahim rejoined his father at Bayana, where from he marched to Punna, only to be defeated and to flee to Orissa.
30. Ibid; Vol. I. p. 533 cf. *The Successors of Sher Shah,* p.75.
31. Ibid; also *The Successors of Sher Shah.,* p.76. Battle of Chhaparghatta., contest between Adli and Muhammad Shah.
32. *Muntakhabu-T-Tawarikh,* Vol. I. p. 555.
33. *The Successors of Sher Shah,* pp. 75-76.
34. Ibid. pp.76-78.

CHAPTER-V

Hemu and Humayun

While Hemu was preoccupied with the adversaries of Adli in the East, and had liquidated them in Behar as well as parts of Bengal; Sikundur Shah Sur wrested from Ibrahim power at Delhi and was easily discomfited by Hemu's armies under his nephew Mahipal near Alwar. Consequently Ibrahim was forced to flee towards the East, and Sikundar sought refuge in the hills of the North. However he became primarily concerned with the attempts of Humayun to regain his lost kingdom in 1554 A.D. (962 A.H.)

For sometime Sikundur successfully rallied the Afghan nobles under him. He spoke to them this effect :- "I esteem myself as one of you; having thus far acted for the common weal, I claim no superiority. Behlol raised the tribe of Lodi to glory and reputation; Sher Shah rendered the tribe of Sur illustrious; and now Humayun, the Mughal heir to his father's conquest is watching an opportunity to destroy us all, and re-establish his government." He called upon them to be sincere, and set aside private faction and animosties;"so that they could still regain their kingdom."[1]

In this way Sikundur won the loyalty of the Afghans temporarily. But very soon disputes arose amongst them, for honour and places; and "the flames of discord were rekindled, and blazed fiercer than ever." The Afghan confederacy established by Sher Shah, became hollow to the core. Islam Shah had eliminated most of the leading nobles' families and under Adli, Hemu defeated the three main contenders to the Afghan throne. There was a vacuum at the centre. Delhi, Agra and Bayana were the main bone of contention and after having eliminated Adli's adversaries in the East, Hemu was supreme in the heart land of northern India.

As Adli was content with his sojourn in the fort of Chunar, there was a temptation before Hemu to consolidate his power in the (Upper Lower) Gangetic Doab and Mewat. So he gained full control over Etawah, Kalpi, Gwalior and Alwar. Adli had placed at his disposal not only the army, cavalry, and war-elephants, but allowed him to carry the vast accumulated treasure on his elephants. Al-Badaoni had clearly mentioned that much wealth was furnished by Adli, which enabled Hemu to overpower most of the Amirs from the frontiers of Hindustan.[2]

Humayun's return: : Having won the Kabul base from his brother, Humayun advanced through tribal territory to recapture his throne in India. As Sur power had been broken in 1554 due to Islam Shah's death, so Humayun advanced by the Kurram —Bangash route. Adam Khan offered to surrender Kamran, who was blinded and was allowed to go to Mecca where, three years later he died. Thus Humayun adopted a barbarous practice of incapacitating a Prince from becoming a King. His achievements prior to that and subsequently were no better. As rightly pointed out by Dr. Qannugo, as "An Empire — builder of the sixteenth century, the Mughals were too few, the Afghans too many and too obdurate, the Hindus either politically innert or inclined too much towards the Afghans, and the country of Hindustan too vast for a foreign invader like Babur to build a *Mughal Empire* after Panipat."[3] Babur in a brief period of four year's existence in India could only initiate some conquests, but could not consolidate them.

Humayun inherited an unstable empire, and enemies alround. His own brothers were intriguing and the Mirzas ungrateful. The Afghan nobles were only lying low to strike at the first opportunity. Bengal and Behar were as turbulent as before Babur's invasion. And during the Sur inter-regnum the Afghans became ascendent all over northern India; but their decline during Islam Shah and Adli tempted the Mughals to strike again.

By December 1554 Humayun had set out towards Hind.[4] he had with him, at that time, 15,000 horse. Munim Khan was left incharge of Kabul. The Mughal ladies all stayed behind. Bairam Khan along with the boy prince Akbar, joined at Peshawar with a body of veterans from Kandahar. The Mughal army occupied Lahore without much effort and advanced upto Jalandhar and Sirhind. Humayun entered Lahore on 24 February 1556.

Battle of Dipalpur:

At the time of Mughal invasion Punjab was under Tatar Khan, an Afghan Amir, who was obliged to retreat without much fight. The fort of Rohtas, the chief stronghold of the Afghans was evacuated. The Afghans rallied at Dipalpur, under Shahbaz Khan and Nasir Khan. They had about 20,000 men under them, and decided to give battle to the Mughals. According to Jauhar the strength of the Afghans was about 12,000 but Bayazid put that at 20,000.

Hamayun deputed Shah Abul Ma'ali, with a strong force against the Afghans. At the battle of Dipalpur, the Afghans suffered a setback, and the victorious Mughals returned to Lahore.

Sikundur Shah Sur : The Afghans rallied round Sikundur at Delhi, and he despatched Tatar Khan and Hubib Khan with an army of 30,000 horse against the Mughals. Both the armies encamped at Machiwara on the banks of the Sutlej. According to Ferishta, the Afghans, due to the cold weather kindled fire, little thinking that the enemy will take advantage of that. Bairam Khan quickly grasped the opportunity and the Mughals crossed the river and advanced towards the Afghan camp without being discovered when the Mughals threw the arrows round those who were enjoying the fire, disorder ensued. In Ferishta's words, "The Afghans (notorious for blundering) instead of extinguishing their fires, which prevented them from seeing their enemies, who had fair view of them, threw on more wood; and the whole of Bairam Khan's army having crossed the river, fell upon them on all sides, and routed them. The Afghans on this occasion lost all their elephants, their baggage and number of horses."[5]

The defeat of the Afghans at Machiwara demoralised them and they fled pell mell. Sikundar Sur was hardpressed, he was beaten by the Mughals from the North-west; and he could not face the armies of Hemu in the East. Desperately he divided his army in two. One unit was to continue operation against Hemu, and the other numbering 30,000 was determined to make a stand under Tatar Khan Kasi in Sirhind.

Battle of Sirhind : 1555 – However Sikundur Sur stirred once again and gathered a huge force of 80,000 horse and marched in person to oppose the advancing Mughals. Bairam Khan sent urgent summons to Humayun to come to his help; who reached Sirhind on 28 May 1555. Various estimates of the Mughal force are available, Jauhar's under estimate put the figure at 5,000, on the otherhand Bayazid mentions 10,000. According to him Humayun sent Iskander Khan Qazzaq, Mirza Khizr Khan Hazara, Lal Khan Badakhshi, Haider Muhammad Akhtal Begi, Mirak and Khaliq Burdi from Lahore alongwith Bairam Khan.[6] Humayun, to ensure his personal safety withdrew to Jalandar.[7] Both the parties began to fortify and continued to make preparations for a month and a half. Abul Fazl records that Humayun waged a masterly war before the decisive battle for forty-days.[8]

The fateful battle took place on June 22, 1555 Thursday. The Afghans relying on their war-mad elephants "behaved with due bravery and valour;" and the *Irani* (Persian) horses of the mughals took to flight. When Humayun saw that they were likely to lose the battle, he changed the tactics; which altered the situation. Sikundur Sur's army was dispersed and he himself fled towards the Siwalik hills. The Afghans were slaughtered mercilessly and vast booty fell in the hands of the Mughals. According to Dr. Ishwari Prasad, the success of the Mughals was chiefly due to superior generalship, better military tactics and rapidity of movement.[9] So it was hailed as a decisive battle, as it laid bare the road to Delhi and Agra.

Humayun moved very cautiously and sent Sikander Uzbeg to find the conditions at Delhi. When he received the report that the throne was vacant, he moved at the head of army to Delhi, where he again ascended the throne on Tuesday – 23 July 1555, after exile and wanderings of about fifteen years. According to Abul Fazl this event took place on Saturday, July 20, 1555 (lst Ramzan 962).[10]

Realising the importance of Punjab, Humayun appointed Abul Ma'ali as governor but Jauhar on the other hand says that"...he took upon himself the command of the province, thereby superseding the officers left in charge by His Majesty."[11] According to Al Badaoni, Shah Abu-l-Ma'ali was distinguished in ancestry, symmetry of his limbs and the excellence of his valour above all his compeers, so Humayun showed a special favour and boundless consideration to him. In order to pursue Sikundur Sur in the mountains of Siwalik, so far as the confines of the district of Dahmiri, Humayun had sent Pir Muhammad Khan Shirwani.[12] Sikundur kept up the war against the Mughals for three whole months, but was atlast defeated. Even then the Mughals were all along apprehending danger from him. Subsequently when Tardi Bag Khan had been routed at the battle of Delhi by Hemu and he has crowned himself, Bairam and Akbar were busy sefeguarding their rear from Sikundar Sur.

Humayun's death : The ill-fated Mughal emperor could hardly rule for six months, when he met an accident and breathed his last on 26 January 1556. As will be evident from the details given below that there is great discrepancy among the contemporary authorities regarding the date of Humayun's death:-

Authorities	Date of Accident	Date of death
Jauhar	....	11th Rabi I. 963 (This is given only in Stewart's translation. It is not given in any of Mss.)
Bayazid	Friday-evening	Rabi – End of 963.

Authorities	Date of Accident	Date of death
Sidi Ali Reis	Friday	Rabi I. Monday 11th Rabi I Friday (In a Ms. referred to by Beveridge – in JRAS. 1903. p. 121).
Tabqat	7th Rabi I	15th Rabi I
Al-Badaoni	7th Rabi I	15th Rabi I
Ahmad Yadgar	7th Rabi I	11th Rabi I
Ferishta	7th Rabi (Sunset)	11th Rabi I
Amal Saaib	11th Rabi I (evening)	13th Rabi I
Badshahnamah	... ...	13th Rabi I – Sunday
Nafais-ul-Ma,sur	Friday 16th Rabi I	Rabi I 18th Sun-day.

(J.A.S.B. 1905 – p.236)

According to most reliable authorities the death occurred on 13th Rabi-ul-awal; i.e. Sunday the 26th January 1556 A.D. and the accident took place on the preceding Friday.[13]

Humayun's state of mind : In the words of Abul Fazl, "At the time when H.M. Jahanbani, with the assistance of the armies of God, conquered India, Hemu was otherwise engaged, and his vain imaginings did not show them selves."[14] But as soon as Humayun had ascended the throne of Delhi, Hemu turned his attention from his rivals and, with a large force of men and war-elephants from the eastern districts, marched towards Delhi, leaving Mubariz Khan, in Chunar. Abul Fazl only mentions that Mubariz Khan had deputed Hemu to fight against the Mughals and Hemu was readying to give challenge to Humayun in the heartland of northern India.

Although Humayun had regained the lost throne, but it is evident from the details given by Abul Fazl and others that he had premonitions of the inevitable i.e. his coming death. When Akbar obtained permission to go to the Punjab, Humayun referred to his coming departure of the world of holiness. From Bayazid's account it appears that he had come to form a poor opinion of the world and was much pained by human wickedness and ingratitude. He had avowed that "if he succeeded in reconquering his ancestral dominion, he would retire from the world, leaving everything to the care of his son and spend the remaining days of his life in the company of pious and learned men."[15]

Although Humayun's son was a minor, and the Mughal ladies were at Kabul, yet he could not help giving expression to his feelings. He also used to visit old graves and sepulchres, in and about Delhi, and his mind was afflicted with a desire to depart to the other world. On the day of accident Humayun had gone up to the roof of Sher Mandal (an old building of Sher Shah in Purana Qila), which he used as a library, and had shown himself to the crowd assembled below on the fateful day.[16]

Date of Accident : Despite varying narratives of different authorities on Humayun's death and the accident Abul Fazl is definite that it occurred on 11th Rabi I i.e. Friday, 24th January 1556 A.D. This is corroberated by the testimony of *Katibi-Rumi,* the Turkish Admiral Sidi-Ali-Reis. He was in Delhi on that day and was also reported to be present at the last audience with the King. His words are : "...Humayun had given audience of on Friday evening, when upon leaving castle of pleasure, the *Muezin*, announced the *Ezan*, just as he was descending the staircase. It was his want, whenever he heard the summon, to bow the knee in holy service. He did so now, but unfortunately fell down several steps, and received great injuries to his head and arm."[17]

Consequently everything was confusion in the palace. For two days they kept the matter secret. It was announced to the outer world that the King was in good health and even alms were distributed amongst the poor. On the third day however, that was on Monday he died of his wounds. But Sidi Ali Reis' version of the date of death has not been corroberated, as Humayun died on Sunday i.e., two days after.

Beveridge in a note on Abul Fazl's account has questioned even the presence of a Turkish Admiral, As Caghatin Khan because there was no Mughal general of that name either in Humayun's reign or Akbar's ! He had come from Gujarat and given audience on Friday as that was the day, Humayun used to hold receptions, and granted interviews.

The date of accident has been confirmed as 24th January, unless as Beveridge has pointed out "it can be established astronomically that Venus did not rise on Friday, 24th January 1556."

Place of accident and mode of fall:

It was a sheer chance that Humayun met his end in a building associated with his arch enemy, Sher Shah. The building was an octagonel one of red stone and had two storeys. But the first part is now solid, i.e. has no room in it. It has inside stairs leading upto the second storey, which is an octagonal room filled with nicheo (*taq*) which perhaps were used as bookshelves. they opened out in the body of the roof, so that *Humayun fell through* the roof rather than off it. He certainly did not fall over the parapet.

What exactly happened at the time of the accident can never be known, but the following version left by Abul Fazl is the most authentic:

"... ... At the beginning of the evening he rushed to descend and when he came to the second step, a reciter (*muqri*) by name Miskin (wretched), raised an untimely call to prayer. His Majesty, out of respect to the call, wished to sit down where he was. As the steps (*darjat*) of the stair (*Zina*) was sharp (*tez*) and the stones slippery (laghzanda) his blessed foots caught in the skirt of his robe at the moment of sitting down and his good staff slipped. He lost his feet and fell upon his head, his right temple receiving a severe blow, so that some drops of blood issued from his right ear ...."[18]

According to Al Badaoni too Humayun fell from the roof of his palace suddenly, as he was coming down and the *mu'azzin* uttered the call to prayer and he bent out of respect for the *Azan*. The layalists apprehensive of the consequences tried to conceal the dreadful occurrences. In the meantime they sent messangers to the boy prince Akbar. In the words of Abul Fazl, "with extreme prudence they kept this life-destroying event from the public for seventeen days." It was only on 11th February 1556, that *Khutba* could be recited in the name of Akbar in *absentio*, the very day when Humayun's death was made public.

On one occasion during the seventeen days the loyalists got dressed up Mulla Bekasi in the clothes of the deceased and brought him out on the top of the terrace and showed him to the public as he resembled Humayun in appearance. According to Abul Fazl "when the sad misfortune was made known a great disturbance and trouble, such as was natural at a crisis like this, arose." The loyalists at the capital were very much apprehensive, as they did not know what to do. In the words of Sidi 'Ali Reis they were" in the greatest consternation" It was on his advice that concealment of death for seventeen days and impersonation by Mulla Bekasi was decided upon. Humayun's death marked a serious crisis in the Mughal history once again. Hemu with his army was knocking at the gates of Agra. Akbar was just a boy of thirteen years, the Doab was desolated by famine, the army was small and the empire was surrounded allround by adversaries. Although no names have been mentioned, it is clear from the records that Sikundur Sur was threatening from the north – i.e. the Siwalik hills and Hemu was in the South-East of Delhi. Although Tardi Beg had assumed charge of the administration, but his writ did not lie much. He was busy sending messages to Akbar expressing his loyalty and devotion.

Sikundur Sur : Akbar and Bairam Khan moved towards the hills in order to extirpate the Afghans leader Sikundur, who was stated to be in Mankot and its neighbourhood. But when they learnt of the fatal fall of Humayun and his death, they returned to Kalanaur. Delhi was already under Tardi Beg Khan; Agra was put under Iskandar Khan Uzbeg; Sambal was incharge of Ali Quli Shaibani; Sarkar Kalpi was under Abdullah Khan Uzbeg; Mewat was looked after by Tardi Beg Khan; Aligarh was administered by Kol Jalali; Haider Muhamad Khan was administering Bayana. Being a boy, Akbar could not assert his authority, so he made over all affairs of state and finance to Bairam Khan. The Mughal position in India was far from secure. Beveridge in his footnote has made interesting comments on Abul Fazl trying to prove to his own satisfaction that the death of Humayun was a blessing in disguise, because it gave scope for Akbar's development. According to Beveridge it is absurd to find him admitting that Akbar did nothing for sometime and left everything to Bairam Khan. Of course a boy of fourteen years could not do otherwise. He had no appetite for reading and learning to write. He is reported to have devoted himself to pleasures of the table.[19] Khafi Khan also mentions about Akbar's devotion to pleasure in his boyhood and his submissiveness to Bairam.

Bairam Khan after assuming reins of administration lost no time in eliminating his adversary Shah Abu-l-Maali, Abul Fazl has given a vivid description as to how he was chained and forced to surrender. In his words "This was the first head of game that fell into fortune's net." This did not provoke any reaction "as Shah Abul Maali was unpopular due to his hot-temper and over – ambitions".

Next came the turn of Sikunder Sur, who was passing his time in the Siwalik hills and was haranguing the Moghuls. He kept up the war for three whole months. At this time Raja Ram Chand came from Nagarkot and paid respects to the Mughal prince Akbar. As the rainy season had set in so the Mughal army reached Jalandhar, and remained there five months.[20]

According to Abul Fazl, "During the time that the camp was at Jalandhar Kamal Khan Gakhar, son of Sultan Sarang, younger brother of Sultan Adam, warmly followed up the old loyalty, and attained the blessing of kissing the threshhold. He became the recipient of princly favours, and was included in the list of officers. *He did good service in the war with Hemu* and Mankot etc., and became the object of special attention from H.M. the Shah-inshah."[21]

Revolt in Kabul : When the news of the death of Humayun reached Kabul, M. Sulaiman and his son M. Ibrahim, due to the confusion allround and due to the immaturity of the successors, laid claim to sovereignty. In the words of Abul Fazl "he changed duties into disobedience "and indulged in rebellion. But after seige of the fort of Kabul, the rebel Sulaiman Mirza was induced to retire on receiving assurances. In actuality Kabul remained under the nominal government of Mohammed Hakim, Akbar's younger brother, and the actual administration of Munim Khan, the minister as well as the governor of Kabul.

India in 1556 : When Akbar proclaimed his accassion at Kalanaur, he could not be said to possess any definite kingdom. The small army under Bairam Khan had a precarious task in Punjab, threatened on one side by the Afghans under Sikundur Sur and on the other side by rebellions Sulaiman Mirza in Kabul, which was for all purposes on independent principality. In India Bengal was under Afghan rule; the Rajputs had recovered from the shock and devastation imposed by Sher Shah. Malwa and Gujarat had thrown off allegiance to Delhi. The wild region of Gondwana (Madhya Pradesh) recognised none as their sovereign. Further South, the Deccan states of Khandesh, Berar, Bidar, Ahmadnagar, Golkanda, Bijapur were governed by their own rulers. In the North the border states of Kashmir, Sind and Baluchistan enjoyed perfect freedom. Even near about Delhi, Sambhal was under Shadi Khan, an Afghan, who was one of the Amirs of Adli. Mewat was firmly under Haji Khan Mewati, an ally of Hemu. Khan Zaman was about to dislodge him from Sambhal when news reached the Mughals that Hemu was near at hand making preparations to attack Delhi.

In the words of Abul Fazl, "As yet the arranging mind was not at rest about the doings of Iskander, and it was watching the commotion at Kabul, when news came to Jalandhar on 31 Mihr, divine month – 8 Zi-Hajja (13th October 1556) of the arrival of *Hemu in whose brain the ambition of sovereignty was stirring ...*"[22]

In actuality the news, which was received on 13th October 1556, must have been of Hemu's great victory in the battle of Delhi on 6th October 1556 and his accession to the throne before 13th October. Abul Fazl reference to "ambition of sovereignty" is significant. This will be fully corroborated by the decisive battle won by Hemu at Delhi and the flight of Tardi Bag.

Mughal discomfiture : Much has been written on the achievement of the first two Moghuls, by Abul Fazl and Al-Badoni, followed by others. They cannot be accused of having written in superlative and unduly praise worthy terms. But it is a pity that biographers of Babur and Humayun, have also toed the same line and lavished unqualified praise on both of them. But as more and more research is done on the achievements of the Afghans, Sher Shah, Islam Shah and Hemu, the too generalized histories of the first two Mughal emperors, fade into insignificance.

Babur had hardly four years time, only to fight a few battles to establish his rule, but he had no time to consolidate that. He was forced to rely on the Afghan nobles cooperation and the support given by Indian Muslim already domiciled in India. Humayun had a shaky start and utterly failed to tackle even his own brothers; between whom the new kingdom was divided. Humayun became the nominal sovereign of northern India; his younger brother, Kamran, became lord of Kabul, Kandhar, Ghazi and the region near the Indus. He was hostile to Humayun and proved to be his worst enemy. It was only after five years that Humayun with the help of the then Persian Shah, succeeded in winning back Kandhar and Kabul from his brother. The tribes men killed Humayun's other brother Hindal. Even Kamran was subsequently forced to leave his helpers on the west bank of Indus and take refuge with Islam Shah. Ultimately he was forced to surrender and was blinded. He was allowed to go to Mecca where, three years later, he died.[23]

Although Humayun had succeeded in regaining his lost throne at Delhi, he could not survive more than six months. in the words of Olaf Caroe, former Governor of the North-West Frontier Province during the last two years before the trausfer of poner in 1947, "He (Humayun) was never an effective King, and like Babur his connection with the frontier was limited to making passage through it."

After 1552 Humayun did attempt to do something to control Peshawar and the Khaibar route, but no sooner had the Badshah left than Khan Kajju invested Bagram (Peshawar) with a strong force and only drew off, because he could not take it without artillery.

The point of substance is "that during the twenty five years that elapsed from the death of Babur to that of Humayun the whole of the trans-Indus area, including the Peshawar Valley and the plains as well as the hill tracks, was beyond Mughal control"[24]

Kamran who held Kabul for sometime had his own schemes and his authority at Peshawar was limited to what the tribals could allow him. The Bangash route was disordered. The Sur's authority lay only east of Bannu, and their last outpost was the newly built fortress at Rohtas. The tribal area remained unsubdued. According to Olaf Caroe, "There was in fact no Mughal empire in the Pathan plains or hills in the days of Babur, Kamran or Humayun..."[25] Even Sher Shah failed to advance so far; his kingdom touched the Indus only east of Bannu. The Sur frontier fortress was at Rohtas. The fort was completed in ten years. Sher Shah ordered its construction, Todarmal Khatri of Lahore executed the task and it was in the middle of Islam Sah's reign that it must have been constructed. In the words of Olaf Caroe, although Sher Shah lies buried in Bihar, at Sahasram, where he grew up and first attained fame. "But his real monument are the old citadel at Delhi and the fortress of Rohtas, looking north beyond the Jihlam."

Even above all the roads, serais, monuments, is the tradition of building an army of elephants, troopers and the Pathan. The remarkable success that he achieved during his short reign of five years, was carried to fruition by Hemu, when he won twenty-two battles for Adil Shah. The technique followed by him, is resplendent by the detailed accounts left by Abul Fazl and Al-Badaoni.

Note and References

1. Neamutullah: trs. Dorn pp. 172-173.
2. *Muntakhabu-T-Tawarikh.*, Vol. II. p.6.
3. *Sher Shah and His Times.* p. 413.
4. *Akbar* p.28. According to Vincent Smith Humayun had started for India in the middle of 1554: also cf. *Gul Badan: Humayun-Nama.* pp. 51-52.
5. *The Rise of Mahomedan Power*, Vol. II. pp. 184-190.
6. Jauhar : p. 156.

7. Prasad. Dr. Ishwari; *Humayun*, p. 345.
8. *Akbarnama*, Vol. I p. 631.
9. *Humayun*; p. 350.
10. *Akbarnama*; Vol. I. p. 634.
11. *Memoirs of Humayun.*, p. 171
12. *Muntakhabu-T-Tawarikh.*, Vol. II. p. 2.
13. *Akbarnama*, Vol. I pp. 654-655.
14. *Akbarnama*, Vol. II. p. 45.
15. Prasad, Dr. I., *Humayun*, p. 54.
16. *Humayun-nama*; by Gulbadan; Introduction by Mrs. Beveridge p. 54.
17. Vambery's translation: *Travels and Adventures*, Luzac; 1899, p. 55.
18. *Akbarnama*, Vol. I. p. 657.
19. Ibid. Vol. II. p. 26. also fn. 2. p. 26.
20. *Muntakhabu-T-Tawarikh*, Vol. II., pp. 4-5.
21. *Akbarnama*, Vol. II. p. 38.
22. Ibid. p. 45. According to Abul Fazl's estimate the total strength of the Afghan forces under Hemu's cammand came to 50,000 eovalry 1000 elephants, 51 canons and 50 falconets.
23. Olaf Caroe: *The Pathans*, 550 BC – A.D. 1957.
24. *Ibid.*, Olaf Caroe; *The Pathans*, 556 BC – A.D. 1957 pp. 194-196, Oxford University Press, Karachi, 1975. London 1958.
25. Ibid., p. 196.

CHAPTER-VI

Battle of Delhi and Accession.

A pertinent question arises, where was Hemu, what was he doing, at the time of fatal accident and death of Humayun? Abul Fazl has recorded that Hemu was ordered by Adli to oppose Humayun who had come to regain his lost empire.[1] It implies that Hemu was holding the field and command of the Afghan army right from June-July 1555 A.D. and was ready to take full advantage of the situation. Other historians have also corroborated the same. Al Badaoni has stated that when Khan Zaman was making preparations to dislodge the enemy, i.e. Shadi Khan, the Afghan, who was one of the Amirs of Adli from the district of Sambhal, "letters came from Dilhi, Agra, and Atawa (Etawah), saying that Hemu with a murderous army, and elephants and much wealth furnished by Adli, having swept before him the Amirs from the frontiers of Hindustan, had arrived close to Dihli with the intention of offering battle."[2]

Vincent Smith has also written in his biography of Akbar, that when Humayun met with the fatal accident, Hemu remained in the field on behalf of Adli, to prevent Akbar from taking possession of his father's kingdom.[3] Both Akbar and Bairam Khan at that time were pitched against Sikundur Sur, who continued to harass the Mughals from the northern Siwalik hills and could have cut off their line of communication with Kabul.

Hemu's preparations : The Mughals were being driven out from Etawah, Kalpi, Agra and Sambhal. A force of the Mughals, under Sekunder Khan Uzbek, and Kobad Khan Gunk, who were at Agra, unable to maintain themselves Hemu, returned to Delhi, and established a liasion with Tardi Beg Khan. The latter sent express messages to all neighbouring and *Sarhadi* Mughal Chiefs to come to his aid at Delhi.

According to Abul Fazl, "the officers (Mughals) who had been deputed to these provinces assembled at Delhi. Tardi Beg Khan became the arranger of the different bodies, and made preparations for giving the battle. He heartened every man by language which might give comfort to the discontented. Many brave and zealous men came in from the districts, but Ali Quli Shaibani, who was engaged in Sambhal in putting down some despicable Afghans, could not join the imperial servants."[4]

Shadi Khan joins Hemu : While informal coronation proceedings were going on at Kalanaur and Delhi was in utter confusion, Shadi Khan of Sambhal defied Ali Quli Khan. He fell upon Muhabbat Khan, Latif Khan, and Ghiasu-d-din and routed them. According to Abul Fazl, "These incapable ones fought without method and let slip and reins of readiness. Latif Khan and a number of others were drowned. When Ali Quli Khan started to attack Shadi Khan, after crossing the river Ruhab (Ramganga), he received an urgent message from Delhi that Hemu was coming with large preparations and that he should come immediately to help him."[5]

Al-Badaoni also specifically mentions that Hemu was moving towards Delhi with a huge army, elephants and treasure furnished by Adli. The Mughal generals viz. Sikundar Khan Uzbeg, Quja Khan Kemb, Abdullah Khan Uzbeg, Haidar Muham Khan, from Agra, Etawah, Kalpi and Bayana alongwith Budukhshy, Ali Quli Khan, Indigany, Meeruk Khan Kelehy and others from the *sarhadi* areas (frontiers) rushed to Delhi to join Tardi Beg Khan, in order to oppose Hemu. Tardi Beg Khan prepared his army for opposing Hemu in Delhi and having received help from other officers, made arrangements for battle. In Abul Fazl's words, "He both made his own heart strong in courage, heartened those who were deficient."

Battle of Delhi : According to the details available, of the battle fought by Hemu, against the Mughals at Delhi, Hemu with his huge army encamped near Tughluqabad.[6] While Hemu had all his equipments the Mughal officer assembled and deliberated how to combat him. Many of the brave men from motives of prudence, and some out of cowardice, were not willing to flight. At length they all decided upon giving battle and all girded upon loins of courage to face the inevitable.

Abul Fazl has given a detailed account of Hemu's preparations and his imaginings of capturing Delhi. According to him the victories gained by Hemu, whom he had the audacity to call "wretch" against the opponents of Mubariz Khan, had emboldened him when the news of the unavoidable events of Humayun's death "reached the province, he (Hemu) out of short-sightedness, took into consideration the confusion of the time and had the audacity to determine that he would give battle to the subline army of H.M. The Shahinshah for whom the divine aid is security." He further adds that the youthful years of Akbar were another "cause of increasing his courage." Moreover "the abundant wealth, and the numbers of soldiers and munitious of war, which had been left by so many rulers of India, *added to his boldness and daring,* as also did the evacuation by victorious (?) officer of the cities and towns of the dominions. At length he set off on his *evil enterprise* with 50,000 cavalry, 1000 elephants, 51 canons, and 500 falconets."[7]

Hemu advanced towards Delhi via Etawah, Kalpi, Agra and Bayana, and the so called victorious Mughal Officer, evacuated those places without a fight. Only Iskandar Khan Uzbeg resisted. Hemu laid seige to Agra, captured its treasure and equipment and having reduced that proceeded to Delhi.[8]

All sorts of nasty things have been written about Hemu by contemporary Muslim chronicles. It has been alleged, out of sheer imagination, by Neamutullah that he vowed, in case he should reduce Delhi, to embrace Islamism; but this bliss not being destined to him by fate, he violated his vow, and remained in eternal misery. But the subsequent martyrdom of Hemu's saintly father at the hands of Mughal general in 1557 January, on refusal to change his religion, does not lend any credence to such a conjecture. It has also been asserted by such prejudicial chroniclers that he (Hemu) often assumed a very insolent behaviour towards the Afghans, inviting the greater part of the army officers to dinner and setting himself upon a raised seat, to which no hand could reach; in that posture he gested with the Afghans, and bade them eat, and salute him as Heemon Shah. There was nothing unusual in such a posture, that showed his popularity among the Afghans and the fraternity. This was the finest example of Hemu's catholicity of heart and a proof of his religious tolerance. In the army he knew no distinction of creed or religion.

According to some chroniclers Hemu's high posture, annoyed some of the Afghan nobles, and they decided to desert him at the next opportunity. After the victory at Delhi, the only battle fought by Hemu was at Panipat and in that there was no desertion by Afghan nobles or generals. The role of Haji Khan Mewati even after Panipat and the sacrifice of Shadi Khan Sambhali at that famous battle lends credence to their loyalty and devotion. The so-called defection of the vanguard of Hemu's artillery was also a story planted to belittle his achievement, as artillery played lesser part in that battle, it was archery that played havoc.

Hemu's victory : At length Hemu's vast army arrived near Delhi, on 24 Mihr, Divine month of the first year, corresponding to Tuesday 1 Zihajja 963, i.e. 6th October 1556. He occupied that vast camping ground in and around Tughlaqabad fort, which is still in ruins. According to Abul Fazl, "Many of the brave men from motives of prudence, and some out of cowardice, were not willing to fight." But there were others in the Mughal army, who were prepared to give their lives for fame, and to whose loyal minds the battle field was more attractive than the banquet hall. These regarded the opportunity as a boon and were ready to engage.[9]

In view of the uncertain and perilious situation, Tardi Beg Khan, without waiting for Ali Quli Khan's arrival, decided to give battle. He collected all the officers, who had taken refuge in the capital – Delhi and drew up for battle. He moved out from Delhi towards Hemu's camping ground at Tughlaqabad, 5 miles East of Qutub Minar, on 7th October 1556.[10] Fredrick Augustus, Count of Noer, in his work on Akbar, Vol. I. published in 1890, has raised some doubt about the date of battle. According to him it was "shortly after accession of Akbar." But if that could be true then Hemu would have ruled Delhi for eight months and not only twenty-nine days before his martyrdom in the battle of Panipat. However Augustus categorically states that after having routed Tardi Beg, Hemu possessed himself of the ancient capital and entered it as King under the capricious title of Raja Vikramajit.[11]

Hemu's Army

1. Hemu —
   I/C Centre and
   the left wing.
2. Shadi Khan Sambhali
   from Sambhal
3. Haji Khan Mewati
   from Mewat
4. Rai Hussain Jalwani
   of Kalpi-Orai.
   I/C Vanguard and the

Mughal Army

1. Tardi Beg Khan

I/C Centre.

2. Afzal Khan
3. Ashraf Khan
4. Pir Muhammad*
5. Haider M. Khan.

Right Wing.

6. Qasim Makhlis
7. Haider Bakshi
8. Ali Dost Khan Bachozi
9. Iskander Khan.

Left Wing

10. Abdullah Uzbeg.
11. Quja Khan.
12. Lal Khan.

Abul Fazl has unequivocally praised the disposition of Hemu's army. In his words, "On the side of the enemy also the troops were drawn up *in martial style,* and they came forward and made manful endeavours. The heroes on both sides cast the thought of life from their hearts, and did great deeds."[12] Due to the spirit of the Mughal vanguard and left wing of the army of the Mughals, the initial victory was gained by them and Rai Jalwani died fighting.

The action began from the side of the Mughal, whose vanguard attacked the right wing of Hemu's army and his vanguard. The onslaught was launched by the commanders of the

---

*Pir Muhammad Khan Shirwani had come from the imperial camp with a message to Tardi Beg Khan, and remained with the army.

Mughal vanguard, viz. Abdula Uzbeg and Iskander Khan, in charge of the left wing as well as Lal Khan of Badakhshan. They swept the ranks of Hemu's army before them, and pursued them as far as the towns of Houdal and Palwal. They succeeded in taking much spoil also. Al Badaoni's statement about this incident in slightly different from other accounts and does not appear to be correct.[13]

According to Abul Fazl "400 noted elephants, were taken away as the spoil, and Rai Hussain Jalwani, a leading man among the enemy, (Hemu's side) was overwhelmed in the ocean of annihilation. More than three thousand of the ill-fated foe descended in the fight to the dust of non-existence."[14] Al Badaoni clarifies the position further, when he records, "But Hemu, who with elephants huge as mountains had remained apart from the fray in the centre of the army, shouted out just as Haji Khan came up from the direction of Alwar, and then attacked Tardi Beg Khan; and in a single charge swept him, before him, but he did not pursue the Mughals." In the evening at the prayer time, when the Amirs of the Mughal army returned form their pursuit of the left wing of Hemu's army, they saw that Hemu had himself settled down there, after having "drawn out softly from the city of Delhi." took immediately to flight. But Hemu forbade his men to pursue them.[15]

According to Neamutullah, Hemu selected three thousand horse and some of his best elephants, which he retained near this own person in the centre, and during the heat of battle, he charged Tardi Beg Khan with such impetuousity, that he was compelled to quit the battlefield and concede victory to Hemu. Abul Fazl due to his own prejudices and over anxiety to exalt the army of providence, accuses Hemu of being proud, and joining "extreme daring to craft" by following feline stratagems." According to him "Hemu collected 300 chosen elephants and a body of life-sacrificing men, and separated them from the rest of his army and awaited the moment for flight or for fight." When Tardi Beg Khan's generals were busy pursuing the left wing of Hemu's army, and had only a small force at his disposal, "The cunning Hemu saw this opportunity and attacked them."[17] The Mughals took to fight and even their generals Pir Muhammad as well as Tardi Beg Khan finding all was lost took to heels. According to some chroniclers, Pir Muhammad Khan had been sent by Bairam Khan, possibly, with a secret brief, to thwart Tardi Beg's efforts at achieving a decisive victory over the Afghans in the absence of the Regent.

The soldiers of the army of the Providence, and their veteran generals were routed, the Mughals took to flight and the city of Delhi surrendered. Hemu emerged victorious and entered the city in triumph. According to Al Badaoni. "Then Hemu in Delhi gave himself the title of Bikramajit, who was a great Raja in Hindustan, from whom the people of Hind take their era, he lived 1600 odd years ago."[18]

Flight of Mughal generals : Khan Jaman remained on the other side of the river and was not able to form a junction with them. When he learnt that Tardi Beg Khan had fled towards Sirhind, he also, by way Mirat'h (Meerut) joined the fleeing army. According to other versions, hearing of the defeat of the Mughals, he stopped marching towards Delhi, and proceeded to Nowshera, with an intention to join the boy king Akbar who was perplexed at the news. He resigned all his powers to Bairam Khan, his tutor guardian and left him to retrieve the affairs. He also assured him of fullest confidence and promised not to pay attention to any of the malicious accusatious against him.

Abul Fazl ascribes defeat of the Mughal forces to the inactivity of Pir Muhammad. According to him, "this (fall of Delhi) happened by fate for purposes known to God alone, or it was brought about by evil design on the part of Maulana Pir Muhammad Shirwani."[19] In his view Tardi Beg did his part well; by making his own heart strong in courage, and heartened those who were deficient, although he had lost his *jagirs* in the Doab and Meerut to the Afghans.

Bairam Khan held Tardi Beg Khan to be responsible for the defeat, although he called him "Toqan", i.e. "Elder brother". He even accused him of treachery, and succeeded in impressing that on the emperor's mind by bringing Khan Zaman, and many others, as witnesses to substantiate his accusations. This enabled him to obtain a sort of permission to put him to death. According to Al Badaoni at the time of afternoon prayer Bairam Khan went to the house of Tardi Beg Khan, and taking him with him, brought him to his own abode into the tent, and afterwards at the time of evening prayer he rose up on the pretence of performing the ablutions, and gave some men, who were held in readiness for the purpose, the signal to slay him. So they made an end of Tardi Beg Khan.[20] Next morning Khwaja Sultan Ali, Mir Munshi, and Khanjar Beg, a relation of Tardi Beg Khan, who were also suspected of treachery, were got imprisoned. They however regained their liberty after some time. Abul Fazl once again emphatically charges Tardi Beg Khan of too rashly evacuating Delhi on Hemu's approach, after some unsuccessful fighting.[21]

Mughal dilemma : Bairam Khan fully realised the gravity of the situation after Hemu's victory in the battle of Delhi. After 6-7th October 1556, some of the Mughal grandees advised retirement to Kabul. But the Khan Khana was equally alive to the uncertain situation there, from where the Mughal ladies were being evacuated to seek asylum in Lahore. But Lahore was safe only till Sikundur Sur was not ready to challenge the Mughals once again. He was poised for another attack from the Himachal Sivalik Hills.

Akbar being only a boy of thirteen years reposed all his trust and hope in Bairam Khan and honoured him with the title of Khan Baba. In return he received assurances of faithfulness, loyalty and devotion. The task before Bairam Khan was extremely difficult, because when he summoned a council of Mughal grandees, the majority were of opinion "that as the enemy's force consisted of more than a hundred thousand horse, while the royal army scarcely could muster 20,000, *it would be prudent to retreat to Kabul.*" Bairam Khan opposed that tooth and nail. Akbar too favoured stay in India and fight for that. Ultimately their view prevailed.

The prompt execution of Tardi Beg Khan had a salutary effect on the other Mughal grandees, and they could not express their indignation openly. They realised that Bairam Khan meant business. Ferishta too has toed the line of Al-Badaoni and Abul Fazl.

Akbar was informed of this drastic step only after it has been accomplished. According to Ferishta's narrative Akbar was acquainted with the fact that "lexity at such a crisis would lead to dangerous consequences, as the only hopes left to the Mughals, at the present moment, depended on every individual exerting himself to the utmost of his power." Akbar was thus convinced that "had Tardi Beg Khan not been executed by way of example, such was the condition of the Mughal army, and the general feeling of those foreigners, that the old scene of Sher Shah would have been acted over again."[22]

Accession to the throne : Hemu's victory at Delhi was decisive and he at once set upon consolidating the same. In victory he acted with restraint and did not take advantage of the flight of Mughal generals. Apprehending confusion and indiscipline in his own ranks, Hemu regarded that strange event — i.e. Tardi Beg's flight — as a trick of the enemy, and so he did not pursue him. Al-Badaoni has emphatically written that Hemu entered Delhi and increased his arrogance, so that intoxication became madness. He gave himself the title of Bikramajit.

The accounts of Hemu's accession to the throne are meagre and shrowded in prejudicial language. The contemporary chronicler in order to please the Mughal emperor and maintain the continuity of Akbar's rule, tried to belittle his achievement by calling him bad names and not recording his accession.

It is evident that prior to Humayun's death and Akbar's nominal accession, even coronation at Kalanaur Hemu was acting on behalf of Adli. No doubt the vast army, the war-elephants, the cavalry and above all the accumulated treasure of the Surs was placed at his disposal. It should be evident even to the casual reader that such a vast army, giving margin to exaggeration by Muslim chroniclers, with elephants and horses, could not be fed and maintained without ample money. Hemu did the wisest thing possible in an anarchical state in 1556. He loaded the entire treasure on the war elephants, so that he had not to depend on any *kiledar* or the governor of a fort for money.

Although the magnificent victory attained by Hemu at Delhi was providential, but the preparations he was making ever since

.Humyun's death on 26 January, 1556, made that inevitable. And as Adli was definitely at Chunar, all the time, it was but natural that Hemu had to act on his own behalf. There was neither any time to take orders from Adli, nor any necessity. Hemu was the non-pareil general, the legendary Vikramaditya and *defacto* ruler of the heart land of Hind. No wonder, having defeated the Mughals decisively at Delhi, *he decided to proclaim himself as the King of Delhi.* There was no question of Hemu's assumption of reins of government in defiance of Adli's orders. The latter had already abrogated his power to him. Had Hemu lived to enjoy sovereign powers at Delhi, Adli would not have questioned him. Frederick Augustus, Court of Noer has applauded Hemu's achievements in these words : "When he had repeatedly defeated had expelled, and killed the Afghan chief of Bengal who seized those. days of disturbance or to attain independence, he subjugated that province in the name of his incapable master." But that could not be repeated at Delhi after Humayun's death. So the Count of Noer, had gone to the extent of imagining that Hemu's accession to the throne occurred shortly after accession of Akbar.[23] Although the possibility of such a long spell of rule prior to Panipat does not appear to be true. But it is definite Hemu during this period i.e. from January to November, was *defacto* ruler and became *dejure* from 6th October onwards.

Vincent Smith has categorically asserted that Hemu not only ascended the throne after the battle of Delhi, but also struck coins.[24] It is evident from his geneological table that he appointed his brother Jujhar Rai as Governor of Ajmer. His nephew, sister's son, Rammayya, Ram Chandra and his nephew Mahipal Rai, grandson Rai Jhande Rao were inducted into the army. It was a pity that he could rule only for 29 days; and due to accidental hit by arrow, Hemu's meteoric rise came to a sudden end.

In such a short time, with danger of a fullfledged war against the Mughals, Hemu could not have thought of anything else than ruling with the greatest catholicity and spirit of toleration. His army consisted mostly of the Afghans, Rajputs and his community men. In such a contingency, it was beyond his comprehension to have thought of subverting the ordinances of Islam.

In this context there is no truth in the allegation of Badaoni that, "when he had done his best there to subvert the ordinances of Islam be came with 1500 elephants of war and treasure without end measure, and an immense army, to offer battle at Panipat."[25] On the otherhand Afghans and Rajputs held him in great reverence and were ready to sacrifice their lives for his sake.

As Dr. Ashirwadi Lal has mentioned in his work entitled "Mughal Empire", Hemu assumption of soverignty, over the throne of Delhi was indeed a bold step. By enthroning himself on the vacant throne in the Tughluqabad fort of Delhi, under the title of Maharaja Hemchandra Vikramaditya, he became the first and only Hindu to occupy the throne of Delhi during the Medieval period of Indian history.

The achievements of a Hindu ruler and remarkable general has been blurred by the prejudicial, false and one-sided statements of medieval Muslim chroniclers. Some of the European writers and their counterpart Indian historians have toed the same line. Few of them like Nirod Bhushan Roy, Dr. Qannugo, and Dr. Ashirwadi Lal have examined the virtues of the forgotten hero, the conquerer of twenty-two battles. Hemu, who had the courage to defend the country against the Mughals, who were for all intents and purposes aliens or foreigners in the land of Hind, had not been given his due. Few have appreaciated and admired Hemu's qualities of leadership and promptitude with which he seized the opportunity of banishing the adventurers and freebooters from across the Indus.

There is lot of truth in Dr. Ashirwadi Lal Srivastava's assertion that if foreigners like Humayun and Sher Shah could advance claims to the sovereignty of India, Hemu, a true son of the soil, a staunch Hindu, secular to the core, had an equally legitimate, and a far greater claim to the throne of Delhi. Even Akbar could not have any better legitimate claims to the crown of India in 1556 A.D. than Hemu. The charge of usurpation of powers vis-a-vis. Adli is also groundless, as Hemu knew his master better than any of the critics and Adli appreciated Hemu equally well. Whatever Hemu did at Delhi in 1556 had veiled consent of Adli, who was content to lead a life of ease and comfort in the Chunar fort.

Note and References

1. *Akbarnama*, Vol. I. p. 659.
2. *Muntakhabu-T-Tawarikh.*, Vol. II. pp. 3-4.
3. *Akbar.*, p. 29. cf. *Jahangir-nama*, trs. A. Rogers, p. 38. according to Jahangir, Hemu had collected a wonderful force after king Humayun's death.
4. *Akbarnama*, Vol. II., pp. 45-46.
5. Ibid : p. 46 & also *Muntakhabu-T-Tawarikh*, p. 5.
6. *Akbarnama.*, Vol. II. p. 47. It lies on the Mehrauli-Badarpur road, about 12 miles from Delhi, now almost part of Delhi. It was founded by Ghiasuddin Tughlaq as his capital in 1321 A.D., completed by 1332 A.D., but was deserted by order of his son, Mahomed Bin Tughlaq in 1327 A.D.
7. *Akbarnama*, Vol. II., p. 47.
8. Ferishta, Briggs trs., pp. 183-190.
9. *Akbarnama*, Vol. I. p. 47.
10. Ibid.
11. *The Emperor Akbar*, Calcutta, 1890., p. 72.
12. *Akbarnama*, Vol. II. p. 48.
13. *Muntakhabu-T-Tawarikh.*, Vol. II. p. 6.
14. *Akbarnama*, Vol. II. p. 48.
15. *Muntakhabu-T-Tawarikh.*, Vol. II. p. 6.
17. *Akbarnama.*, Vol. II. p. 48., also see pp. 29-30. and cf. *The Mughal Court Politics during Bairam Khan's regency* by Iqtider Alam Khan, *Medeival India*, A Miscellany, Vol. p. 26.
18. *Muntakhabu-T-Twarikh.*, Vol. II. p. 7. and fn. -6. according to which his date was 57 B.C. The date of the year in which the writer speaks in 964 A.H. And A.H. is 621. Thus 57+621+964=1642, and the "odd years" of which he speaks are 42.
19. *Akbarnama*, Vol. II. p. 46.
20. *Muntakhabu-T-Tawarikh*, Vol. II. p. 7.
21. *Ain-i-Akbari* : Vol. pp. 318-319 : *M.U.T.* fn. 5. According to the editor Tardi Beg Khan was a noble of importance in the time of Humayun and one of the most *faithless* followers. Blochman's *Ain-i-Akbari-I.* p. 318. He was a *Sunni.* Bairam

Khan was a *Shi'ah*, Badaoni III. p. 190. also *Maasir-ul-Umara* (Vol. I. p. 470).

22. *The History of the rise of Mahomedan Power in India.*, p. 184-190.
23. *The Emperor Akbar.*, Vol. I. pp. 72-73.
24. *Akbar the Great Mughal* : pp. 27-28.
25. *Muntakhabu-T-Tawarikh*; Vol. II. pp. 6-7.

[illegible] and A[illegible]

[illegible]

22. The [illegible] [illegible] (30)

[illegible]

24. [illegible] pp. [illegible]

25. [illegible] pp. [illegible]

[illegible]

CHAPTER-VII

Second Battle of Panipat

Nothing electrifies the mind of the casual student of Indian History than the account of the three battles of Panipat; fought one after the other at the same place between the Afghans and the Mughals. Their importance and significance is unique. While the one ushered in the rule of the Timurids, the Mughals in India in 1526 A.D.; the second one fought by Hemu and the Afghans saved the Mughals from exit and extinction from Hind in 1556 A.D; and the third one fought by the Mughals and the Peshwa led to the defeat of the former by the Afghan invader, Ahmad Shah Abdali in 1761 A.D.

The nature and alignment in all the three historic battles show that the struggle took the shape of a straight fight between Indians, inclusive of Muslims domiciled in India, and the foreign invader. The Mughals succeeded in overpowering the Afghans in the first one; but just escaped defeat in the second; and finally gave way to them in the third one. In short whilst the first one led to the foundation of Mughal dynasty in India, the second one saved them from second exit; but the third and the last one sounded their death, knell.

Out of the three battles, the second one stands most prominently, as the leadership of the Indian army was in the hands of Hemu, the last Hindu king of Delhi. It was due to Hemu's victory at the battle of Delhi, that the Mughals suffered a rout. Emergence of Hemu at the head of a huge army, with immense treasure of the Surs, and with the formidable combination of the Afghans, Rajputs and the rest; along with mountain like war-elephants and a fine cavalry, threw the Mughals into panic. But for the accidental death of Hemu, by an arrow, and the providential victory of the Mughals under Akbar, the history of India would have been different.

Plight of Mughals: The Mughals were in a very tight position. Akbar, a boy of 13 along with his tutor-guardian Bairam Khan, was at Kalanaur, a king without a throne or territory; and threatened by Sikundar Sur in the Punjab and Siwalik hills. At Kabul the Mughal ladies, feeling unsafe, were on way back to Lahore. They could arrive at Mankot in the early quarter of 1557 and went to Lahore when the camp broke, and from there travelled to Delhi on December 7, 1557. Kabul was in revolt with Sulaiman and Ibrahim Mirza, having decided to establish their hegemony. But Munim Khan, the Khan-Khanan with a small force guarded Kabul against him.[1]

"At this time", as recorded by Abul Fazl, "there was great scarcity in the cities and village of India, and there was a terrible famine, in many parts, especially in the province of Delhi. Though they were finding signs of gold, they could see no trace of corn".[2]

Badaoni had also given vivid description of the famine. He had said, that the famine lasted two years, it apparently prevailed during 962 and 963 A.H. i.e. January 1556 — 963 A.H. He was no doubt an eye witness to the famine and has recorded that "the peoples died with bread upon their lips...."[3]

According to Abul Fazl also the great famine occurred in the beggining of the year of accession of Akbar, i.e. January 1556-963 A.H. The capital was devastated and nothing remained but a few houses. An epidemic of plague ensued and spread through most of the cities of Hindustan. Multitudes died. The scarcity and shortage of grain were no doubt aggravated by the devastation and sufferings caused by the assemblage of armies and constant fighting. According to Abul Fazl "Men took to eating one another; some would join together and carry off a solitary man and make him their food."

The economic condition had worsened in a distracted and ill-governed period. The provinces of Agra and Delhi were desolated by an appalling famine caused by widespread failure of the rains, combined with the devastation wrought by two years of continuous warfare. An epidemic plague also ensued and spread through most of the cities of Hindustan. Multitudes died due to that also.

Badaoni had reflected too much on Hemu's indifference to famine conditions. But his very mention of that in connection with the battle at Bayana shows that his reference is at variance with other contemporary writers. As Hemu was in the throes of wars against the erring Afghan Amirs, the army, and its animals had to be fed. But it is too much to say that he valued the lives of a hundred thousand men at no more than a barley corn. Of course in order to maintain law and order, and use his five hundred elephants, he had to feed them upon rice, sugar and butter. There is contradiction in Badaoni's narrative, the people of the provinces of Agra and Delhi were normaly fed on *wheat* cereal, which was not given to animals according to him, only rice was given to the elephants. So Badaoni is the only writer who accuses Hemu for brutality to the human beings, vis a vis the animals of the army and his version seems to be prejudicial and exaggerated.

Abul Fazl only mentions that the famine was raging at the time of accession of Akbar, naturally it must have been due to rain failure. But the near-by province of Alwar-Ajmer-Sirhind from where Hemu hailed, there was no such famine or pestilence. So on the face of it these accounts are exaggerated. Hemu being well versed in the management of the a grain market, could not have been brutal or oblivious to the suffering of the general public.

Hemu's vanguard : Barely three days before the battle of Panipat Bairam Khan, the guardian tutor of boy Akbar, having decided to stay back in India, delivered an inspiring speech to the Mughal grandees, most of them had gathered to pay homage to him, to remain united in the face of common danger. After preliminary preparations the Mughal army moved towards Panipat, the historic battle-field. When news of the same reached Hemu, he is reported to have"... sent his park of artillery, great both in quality and in quantity, in advance of himself, and under the charge of Mubarak Khan and Bahadur Khan who were chief officers of his, to Panipat, which is nearly thirty Kos from Delhi, and set about preparing for battle..."[4]

According to well informed circles, the above park of artillery was not very well guarded and was numerically a weak lot. It was hasty action on the part of Hemu, to have sent such a vanguard, so much well in advance of the main army. When the Mughals, "heard of the arrival of the artillery at the town, they equipped a force composed of active and battle-loving soldiers, such as Lal Khan Badakhshi, M. Quli Uzbeg, and Samaiyi Khan and sent them forward to make an attack". They did not regard the apparent numerical superiority without fear and did not put off the attack for the next day. Without semblance of hesitation or delay they drew up their forces and decided to engage.

According to Abul Fazl, Hemu's vanguard "artillery was captured, and the advanced guard of the enemy fled without fighting."

Badaoni gives slightly different version when he says: "He sent on his artillery before him and — the opportunity presenting itself to a company of the great amirs such as Khan Zaman, Iskandar Khan and others, who were advancing as vanguard, they took it at Panipat after some fighting."[5] But the Afghans, since they were "sick of his usurpation, began to pray for his fall, and in impromptu kept saying thing to this effect: — Welcome a vicissitude even against ourselves," consequently without delay started for Panipat on the morning of Friday, the 10th of the sacred month of Muharam 964 A.H. (1556 A.D); and began fighting.[6]

Badaoni's account appears far from the truth; as it was a fact that the park of artillery with Hemu was numerically inferior and having advanced hastily fell on easy prey to the enemy. And it is too much to say that the officers in charge of the artillery, being Afghans, betrayed Hemu. On the basis of Badaoni's account alone this allegation cannot be fully established. He has only conjectured that, as the Afghans were not satisfied with Hemu's distribution of patronage amongst them, they betrayed. Dr. Ram Prasad Tripathi has rightly said : "It was indeed a fatal mistake of Hemu to have his park of artillery in advance under weak guard."

According to Fedrick Augustus, Count Van Noer, this event occurred on 4th November 1556, when Ali Quli Khan was a little to the South of the plain of Panipat. In his words the capture of Hemu's artillery, was a success which in no mean degree contributed to the Mughal victory on the day of the main battle, i.e. 5th November.[7] But it was not the decisive act, as the accidental death due to the arrow was the last straw.

Hemu's advance : According to Abul Fazl when Hemu learnt of the capture of the park of artillery and the vanguard, "he arrayed his army in three divisions."[8]

1. The right wing was commanded by Shadi Khan Kakar, an Afghan tribe.

2. The left wing by Hemu's sister's son, Ramya, (Ram Chandra Bhargava who was distinguished for bravery).

3. Hemu himself commanded the centre, and marched forward with consummate pride and celerity.

War elephants : Hemu relied mostly on his war elephants, vivid description of which is available by Abul Fazl in these words:

"He took with him the mountain like dragon-mounted elephants, which had been collected by so many Indian rulers, and which by Heaven's decree and for a warning to the superficial and the short-sighted had been brought together for this action in form and substance. Amont them were 500 palmary (Sira) elephants,[9] each of them a paragon for swiftness and dexterity. In might and courage they were examplers and the running of those active athletes could not be called running, for though the race-horse of Iraq' (Arabia), be swift they could not outstrip these elephants. In truth each one of these famous elephants was capable of disordering a large force. They were especially calculated to confuse the onset of cavalry as the horses had never seen such terrific forms."

The author further goes on describing the valour of elephants with the same rhetoric;

"How can the attributes of those *rushing mountains* be strung on the slender thread of words. They ruined lofty buildings by shaking them and they uprooted strong trees. In the hour of battle, and they lifted up man and horse and flung them into the air."

Verse "They advance at a gentle pace, but when they encounter, the strong are as powdered antimony under their feet."[10]

Hemu's Army : Besides 1500 war elephants and a vanguard of artillery park, Hemu "marched in *excellent order* with 30,000 practised horsemen composed of Rajputs and Afghans who, on many occasions, had by their exploits increased his pride and arrogance."[11] In order to hearten the soldiers and the Afghan Amirs, Hemu had given gifts of land, and opened the door of his treasure. Thus he mobilised the valiant fighters. His last-minute preparations, distributions of famous war-elephants have also been acclaimed by the Mughal chronicle, in these words:-

"....Musketeers and cross-bows men were placed on the mountain backs of those enormous elephants, which were furnished with suits of mail (Kazim) and defensive armour, and made ready for war. All the elephants had these war panoplies, and were intrusted to men of war and to courageous drivers. Every one had his place as signal to him."[12]

Each one of the famous elephants had his own name and were assigned to the important leaders as detailed below:

Name of elephants	Assigned to
(i) Ghalib — Jang — (One of the first rate elephants)	Hasan Khan Faujdar.
(ii) Gaj Bhanwar (Whirlpool)	Maikal Khan
(iii) Jor Banyan (a powerful one)	Ikhtiyar Khan
(iv) Fauj Madar	Sangram Khan
(v) Kali Beg	Capan

The last one had in many battles been ridden by Hemu himself, but on the fateful day it was entrusted to a driver of the name Capan. According to Abul Fazl, "Hemu conciliated the Afghan leaders, who were lions of the jungle of war, and were confidants of Sher Khan and Selim Khan, other haughty ones, and made them zealous for battle."

(vi) Hawai — Hemu — It came from Kharmaunda, the district of Kharamanda.

It was the common practice in medieval India that the commander-in-chief of the army or the king in command, was to ride an elephant and be visible to the rank and file, while in action. Hemu followed this practice literally. He was seen in his *howdah* always shouting and encouraging his soldiers as well as Amirs. His inspiring presence and the art of elephant riding was a source of great strength to him and a sure measure of his victory.

Use of elephants : In the Indian armies elephants always formed a very important branch. Whilst in ancient India, the elephant was more on less regarded as sacred and the best (Gaj Uttame) but was also used as a means of transport and mounting in wars. In medieval India, both Hindus and the Afghans perfected the art of elephant warfare. They were not only well trained but also fully armed with lances, spears and armour. Neamatullah, while describing the exploits of Miyan Muhammad Firmulli *hakim* of Oudh, against twenty-four Hindu Rajas, whom he tried to subjugate, says that, "They fought so desperately that their swords became glued to their palm. One of their elephants clad in in a steel cuirass was dragged away; eight maunds of iron were taken off its body..."[13] It was customary to name such well-equipped elephants.

Mast elephants : Having trained mountain like elephants, the Indian rulers began to rely too much on *mast* animals This happened in both the first battles of Panipat in 1526 and 1556 A.D. Under Ibrahim Lodi, while the cavalry numbered only 100,000 the elephants were reported to be near about 10,000. During the course of the first battle of Panipat, whilst the Mughals showed extraordinary dexterity and activity on the eve of the battle, the Afghans were lukewarm and inactive. In the words of Neamatullah, "Apparently he (Ibrahim) wanted to overwhelm his opponent by the momentum of his attack. He had calculated that the trained *mast* elephants forming the spear-head of his advance, would break the Mughal line by means of their almost irresitable impact; the cavalry would then follow and strike with sword and arrow."[14]

But Ibrahim Lodi was simply perplexed at the sight of Mughal forces wagon line, ditches etc. "looming like a row rampart —

and the row of parks, entwining branches of trees, like pylons." He also could not assess the relative strength of the artillery against the elephants. Previously too he had used elephants in campaigns against his enemies, e.g. against the Tomars of Gwalior and drafted a large body of their trained animals, numbering 1000, to face the onrush of cavalry. These were comparable to morning clouds on the march, and were as overwhelming in attack and death — dealing blows as tanks in modern warfare. But Ibrahim Lodi was disillusioned as these animals were demobilised by Mughal artillery and cavalry. The muskets of Babur's artillery, discharging balls intermittently at a distance of three miles, possessed a striking power which rendered the war elephant an encumbrance rather then a source of strength. It can well be imagined how the elephants, struck by the balls, became wild with rage and broke their own ranks, and thus hastened defeat. Thus in points of number of combatants, first battle of Panipat was important in showing how the use of missiles and balls, accompanied by shock tactics, succeeded over obsolete weapons, antiquated technique and *mast* elephants.

Inspite of the past experiences, the Afghans stuck to their love of elephants and during 1553 to 1556 Hemu utilised them in his conquests — the twenty two battles, which he had won. It was due to such swift moving elephants that his armies could dash from Ajmer to Agra, Bayana, Kalpi, Etawah, Chunar, Rohtas and even upto Khawaspur Tanda. If one apportions the time he had to traverse the distances to and from in those days, when roads were limited one must give him full credit for being in the *howdah* for most of the time. It was during his generalship that the armour of the *mast* elephants was improved. He was more cautious and vigilant. It was only a chance that led to his defeat; otherwise with a formidable army under his command, he would have driven out the Mughals out of India for good.

In action : According to Abul Fazl on the fateful day, i.e. Dibadin, the 23rd Aban, Divine month, corresponding to Thursday, 2 Muharram, 964, — 5th November 1556, that the Mughals made certain that Hemu was "boldly approaching."[15] He first of all despatched a large force in advance with elephants in the first rank, marching in single column under the command of Shadi Khan Kakar; who had already distinguished himself in the battle of Delhi and hailed from Sambhal. Badaoni has also stated that the leader of the Afghan Amirs, was Shadi Khan Maswani, whose hopes had been raised high by suitable augmentation and a gift of lands, as well as distribution of wealth.[16]

According to Badaoni, Hemu's army was all dispirited, and who set all his hopes on the elephants, surrounded by his chiefs charged the imperial hosts, and *threw both right and left wings into great confusion.* Then Hemu, bringing up all his mountain — like elephants *to bear upon one point*, charged the centre where the Khan Zaman was stationed.

Abul Fazl also testifies to the panic in the Mughal camp, when he records, that as soon as the Mughals became certain of the immensity of Hemu's preparations, "perturbation found its way into the hearts of imperial servants, through the instrumentality of empty headed babbles, from whom no army is ever free or rather armies of such."[17]

The Mughal vanguard : Badaoni has recorded that "fighting and slaughter began between the Amirs of the vanguard and the hosts of Hemu. The Emperor and the Khan Khanan on that day were drawn up in three division, and kept sending help to one another until news of the victory were received."[18]

The Mughal vanguard according to other sources consisted of 10,000 cavalry, out of which 5000 were experienced veteran soldiers, and they got ready to meet the advancing army of Hemu. Iskander Khan commanded the right flank; whilst the left was led by Abdulla Khan Shaiban, Husain Quli Khan, Shah Quli Mahram and several other young generals. Among other generals who took part on the side of the Mughals were, Muhammad Qasim Khan of Nishapur, who had distinguished himself in the war with Sikandar Sur and served as Harawal, or leader of the Van, under Khan Zaman in the battle with Hemu.[19] Another general, Shah Quli Mahram-i-Baharhi, who was in Bairam's service, distinguished himself in the war, against Hemu's elephant, "thought he did not know who is opponent was."[20] When the driver disclosed the identity of his master Quli Khan spared him and took Hemu's body.

Bairam Khan and Akbar : When the fight began on 5th November 1556, both Akbar and Bairam Khan were at Karnal, ten Kos from Panipat, and advanced towards the battlefield. They halted at a place 5 Kos from Panipat and at that place heard dis-quieting news of good many Mughals having given way but "that fighting was still going on briskly."

Abul Fazl in order to exalt his master, has bestowed undeserved praise on both Akbar and Bairam Khan. According to him "H.M. with a kingly and tranquil countenance placed the helmet of Divine fortune on his head, one cuirass of God's protection on his breast, and the foot of dominion in the stirrup of intent." Similarly Bairam Khan was reported to have moved in front of the ranks, and round the divisions and took measures for preserving the rules of war, and protection of points. On behalf of H.M. the Shahinshah, Bairam Khan distributed promises of favour and anger, and set in order the banquet of battle. But the fact remains that both Akbar and Bairam were far away from the battlefield and did not play any part in the same. It was only when Hemu has been struck by a fatal arrow and fell in his *howdah* that news was conveyed to Akbar and Bairam Khan that the battle has been won. Hemu was captured and his lifeless body brought before them from the battlefield of Panipat. It has been categorically recorded by Abul Fazl in *Ain-i-Akbari* "Though Akbar and Bairam Khan were *near*, they took no part in this battle." On the day of battle Akbar starting from Karnal had reached Sarhunda, 10 miles north of Panipat. The vanguard of the Mughals was under Ali Quli Khan who met Hemu near Panipat.[21]

Hemu's performance : Giving an account of victory Abul Fazl had remarked that when Hemu became aware of the main Mughal army being far off, and only some of the officers having come in advance, "he rapidly marched against them, thinking that if he dispersed these men, who were the choice troops, the rest of his task would be easy. He relied upon the numbers of his experienced troops, and on his many strong elephants, and advanced with immeasurable pride."

It had been recorded by the Mughal chronicler that "the onset of elephants shook the right and left divisions." When Mughal generals like Muhd. Qasim Khan of Nishapur, Husain Quli Khan, Shah Quli Mahram, and L'al khan Badakkshi saw that the horses would not be able to face the elephants, "they fetched a circuit and like famished tigers, sought their prey with blood dripping swords and closed with the foe and overcome him. They hurled firmly — seated riders from their saddles and then despatched them by the dagger-hoofs of swift, fiery horses. Bands of devoted archers came forward on all sides and did yeamonly service." The Mughals under Ali Quli Khan Shaibani had come to a spot "which had a great ravine in front of it, such that even elephants could not cross." They showed such endurance that the elephants retreated from the sides of the centre."[22] In actual fight Hemu relied mainly "on his many strong elephants, and advanced with immeasurable pride."

Hemu proudly rode on an elephant named *Hawai*, which was one of the best, and glanced from side to side at the brave swordsmen, and at the onset of the rank — breaking *Ghazis*. He showed great stratagem together with a band of fierce elephants which his powerful capacity could conceive. Abul Fazl praises Hemu still further, when he says, "He made powerful onsets and performed many valorous acts, and dislodged many strenuous soldiers of the sublime army."[23]

Euloging the grand design of re-conquerring India,the Mughals while preparing themselves to extirpate Hemu, gave an order to arrange fireworks as a treat to the soldiers. They made an image of Hemu, filled that with gunpowder, and set that on fire. Abul Fazl then adds that "on none of these former occasions was there a ruler of India, possessed of such courage, enterprize and plan (as Hemu). On the contrary, they were backward in the management of their own dominions. It was other wise with this visible spirit(?); he was ever meditating the conquest of distant climes and kept hidden in his heart the designs of great expedition. And in truth fortune had favoured Hemu in a way which the rulers of India had not attained to in those former days,..."[24] He had tried soldiers, number of able officers, plenitude of artillery and number of powerful elephants, which could throw any army into confusion. Thus by comparing other Indian rulers with Hemu, Abul Fazl had brought out his greatness and acclaimed him a ruler.

When Sikander Khan Uzbeg pursued the fugitives right upto Delhi, the Mughals captured as many as 1500 elephants. The rest of the equipment could be conjectured from that. Much plunder fell into his hands. Hemu was absolute and had control of all the elephants, etc. of Adli. An immense booty fell into the hands of the enemy, the Mughals.

Ferishta' tribute : According to Ferishta's narrative Hemu began the action with his elephants, in the hope of alarming the enemy's cavalry, unaccustomed to these animals but the Mughals fought so furiously that the elephants threw their own army into confusion. Hemu when struck by an arrow, sunk into his *howdah* from extreme agony. But "Raising himself again, Hemu drew the arrows and with it the eye of the socket, which he wrapt in his handkerchief, and inspite of his painful situation, he continued to fight with unabated courage, endeavouring with the few men who remained about his person, to force his retreat through the enemy's time."[25] And but for accidental death of Hemu by an arrow, his onslaught at the centre would have made a short-shrift of the vanguard of the Mughal army. The well-directed flight of arrows decided the second battle of Panipat. The Afghans and the Rajputs along with Hemu's kinsmen were overpowered by a handful veterans from Central Asia.

Mughal tactics : When the Mughal generals were convinced that their horses were no match for the mad elephants, they hatched a *circuit* plan i.e. made *an outflanking movement*. According to the translator of Abul Fazl's *Akbar-nama*, it probably meant "onfoot", i.e. the Mughals got down from the back of the horses and changed tactics to surround the elephants. The riders had already been hurled down from their saddle and then despatched them by the daggerhoofs of swift fiery horses. The cavalry constituted the strength of the Mughals.

At this critical moment, the Mughals threw a devoted band of archers on all sides, who did signal service. When the elephants retreated from the sides of the Centre, the archers came out in the rear of the Hemu's army "and discharged their arrows and wielded their swords" gave them victory over overwhelming odds. Hemu's traditional mode of warfare was counteracted by the new military strategy.

The fatal accident:

Abul Fazl after exhausting his flowery language has also quoted a verse regarding the fierce battle that took place, He quotes:

"Two armies so collided that they struck fire out of water;
You'd say the air was all crimsoned
Their steel had all become solid rubies", daggers,
"Suddenly', in the midst of the contest,

"An arrow from the bended bow of Diviner wrath reached Hemu's eye, and piercing the socket, came out at the back of his head."[26] In the words of Badaoni too, "Suddenly the arrow of death which no shield can ward off struck his (Hemu's) squinting eye so that his brain passed clean out from the cup of his head, and he became unconscious."[27]

At this time when the victory would have been his, Hemu met with this fatal accident, "Being pierced through the eye with an arrow, he sank into his *howdah* from extreme agony... Raising himself again Hemu drew the arrow and with the eye out of the socket, which he wrapped in his handkerchief, and inspite of the powerful situation, he continued to fight with unabled courage, endeavouring with the few men who remained about his persons to force his retreat through the enemy's line."[28]

Death of Shadi Khan and others:

Shadi Khan Sambhali, who was the chief of the Afghan Amirs on Hemu's side, died fighting. According to Abul Fazl he "was trampled under the feet of the swift horses of fortune's armies."

Badaoni mentions that a general carnage ensued and Shadi Khan Muswani, who was in the van of the army was slain. Abul Fazl has recorded that one Raja Bhagwan Das "one of the leading men and who was distinguished for his bravery in the field of battle was cut to pieces in front of him (Hemu)." Bhagwan Das was no doubt one of Hemu's best generals, and his loss was irreparable. It is a pity that the redoubtable warrior has not yet been identified by any historian.

Recent researches into Hemu's community history and the geneologies have revealed that Ramya, Ram Chander Bhargava, Hemu's sister's son and his seven brothers as well as cousins died fighting. Though no mention has been made, but Hemu's nephew, Mahipal also sacrified his life in the battlefield. It was only after his demise that his son Nathmal, the lone surviver although an infant, was bestowed the Qanungoi of Kanaud by Akbar, through a Firman in 1563 A.D.

From all accounts it is clear that the battle before and after the fatal accident to Hemu was fierce. It was not a cake-walk for the Mughals. But for the fatal accident, Hemu could have been crowned with success. However destiny willed otherwise and after his collapse, the rank and file lost heart and fled. Along with died his nephews and other generals of repute. Their sacrifices deserve equal praise.

Captive Hemu:

With the master lying fatally wounded in the Howdah, the driver of the elephant. "Hawai" found himself in a quandry. Various accounts of the capture have been given. According to Al-Badaoni, "Shah Quli Khan Mahrum happened to meet Hemu's elephant, and the elephant-driver said to him. *Do not kill me ! Hemu is riding upon my elephant*, So they brought him as he was to the camp."[29]

Abul Fazl has also given identical account. According to him when Shah Quli Khan approached the elephant of Hemu, he did not know about the person riding on that. He was more attracted by the elephant, its size and demeanour. The driver apprehending danger to own life disclosed the identity. When Shah Quli Khan learnt of the captive, he was overjoyed, blessed his stars and tossed the cup of joy to the skies. He took the captive elephant and left the battlefield. The author has expatiated on the part played by the driver of the elephant and their importance.

It was quite in keeping with the tenets and the consequences of India in warfare based on the elephant. Although they played an important part in almost all battles, but they afforded their riders as best targets for archers. And they could not be as swift as the horses. As a result of that many battles, which could have been won, were lost by undue reliance on elephants. Good many warriors fell a prey to the vagories of elephants, their flight at the crucial moment; full many a kingdoms had been lost only due to the defection of elephants.

Hemu was no exception. His collapse due to mortal would was a signal for the rout of the army. the elephant, unlike a faithful horse like Chetak, could not drive his master, out of the battlefield. The driver had the ultimate say. His two generals, Shadi Khan Sambhali, Raja Bhagwan Das and his two trusted warrior nephews, Ramya and Mahipal met their glorious end on the battlefield.

Notes and References

1. Gul Badan: *Humayun-nama*: Introduction — See III pp. 56-56. See also Erskine, p. 509 and M.U.T. Vol. II p. 5.
2. *Akbarnama*, Vol. II, pp. 56-57. Also *The Successors of Sher Shah*, pp. 76-77.
3. *Muntakhabu-T-Tawarikh*, Vol. I. pp. 541-542 See also *Asiatic Quarterly Review* for January 1901, pp. 29, 30, and *ibid* for July 1901, p. 103
4. *Akbarnama*, Vol. II. pp. 58-61.
5. Ibid., p. 59.
6. *Muntakabu-T-Tawarikh*, Vol. II, pp. 7-8.
7. *The Emperor Akbar.*, Vol. I. p. 74.

8. *Akbarnama.*, Vol. II. p. 59-61. Also *Smarika*, Rewari, 1989. Geneological Table of Ramya by Dr. Manhar Gopal Bhargava.
9. *Ain-i-Akbari Book Second* : A'n 2. The animals of The Army p. 246. According to Abul Fazl the branded elephants of the Mughal army even at a later date were divided into seven classes:- Mast, Shergir, Sada, Manjhola, Karha, Pandarkuja and Mokal elephants. The monthly allowance for *Mast* elephants was 1,320 *dams* (Rs.33/-). Daily allowance of grain 21/2 *man* per diem. No elephant had more than three servants, a *Mahawat*, a Bho'i, a and a Meth. *Shergir* elephants: Monthly cost 1,100d which was 220 *dams* less than the former. Grain 2 man per diem. Two servants — *Mahawat* and *Bho'i*. Sada elephants: Monthly cost 800 *dams*. Grain 11/2 man per diem. *Manjhola* elephants: Monthly cost 600 *dams*. Grain 1 m. *Karha* elephants: Monthly cost, 420 *dams*. Grain 30 seer. *Ponidarkuya* elephants. Monthly cost 300 dams Grain. 15 Seer per diem. *Mokal* elephants were were formerly not counted. Monthly allowance, 280 *dams*. Under Akbar they began to be taken into account. According to reliable sources there were about 1500 elephants in the Mughal studs.
10. *Akbarnama.*, Vol. II. p. 60
11. Ibid: "Armed to the teeth, sheathed in coats of mail these elephants in battle army formed a solid rampart which could withstand the ceaseless assault of the enemy." cf. N.B. Roy. pp. 85.
12. Ibid.
13. Roy, Nirodbhushan., (trs) *History of the Afghans*, p. 126 also fn: According to Ms Add II, 633 such killing and fighting took place that the blood of the worthless *kafirs* flowed in stream. Eight maunds of steel were taken off the body of an elephant which had broken the shafts and lances.
14. Ibid.
15. *Akbarnama.*, Vol. II. p. 60.
16. *Muntakhabu-T-Tawarikh.*, Vol. II. p. 8.
17. *Akbarnama.*, Vol. II. p. 62.
18. *Muntakhabu-T-Tawarikh.*, Vol. II. p. 8.

19. *Ain-i-Akbari.*, p. 353.
20. *Ibid.*, p. 359.
21. *Ain-i-Akbari.*, Vol. I. pp. 353-359.
22. *Akbarnama,* Vol. II. p. 64: Nirodbhushan Roy on the basis of the Mukhzan has also stated that Hemu's attacks were fierce and violent and the Mughal army could not withstand them; p. 86.
23. Ibid.
24. Ibid., p. 69.
25. *Rise of the Mahomedan Power in India,* Vol. II. pp. 188-189.
26. *Akbarnama.*, Vol. II., p. 56.
27. *Muntakhabu-T-Tawarikh.*, Vol. II. pp. 8-9.
28. *Akbarnama,* Vol. II. p. 64.
29. *Muntakhabu-T-Tawarikh,* Vol. II. p. 9. cf. *The Successors of Sher Shah,* p. 87.

[illegible]

19. [illegible]

20. Ibid., p. [illegible]

[illegible]

[illegible] Nandikeshwar Kay on the basis of the [illegible] [illegible] and the [illegible] [illegible]

[illegible]

Ibid.

Ibid.

[illegible] of India, Vol. II, pp. 129-[illegible]

[illegible]

[illegible] Vol. II, p. [illegible]

[illegible] Vol. II, p. [illegible] The [illegible]

[illegible], p. [illegible]

CHAPTER-VIII

Hemu's Martyrdom.

According to Abul Fazl, the battle of Panipat was so fierce that approximately the number of those who had fallen on the battle-field was calculated at 5,000 the number of those who were trampled down on the roads during the flight, could not be counted. As many as 1500 noted elephants fell into the hands of the Mughals servants. The figure might be exaggerated, as the number of war-elephants was near a bout 500 only. Abul Fazl records further, "whilst every one of the heroes was being brought into the presence and was receiving rewards temporal and spiritual, Shah Quli Khan brought in Hemu bound."

Thereafter Bairam Khan Khan — Khanan begged Akbar to slay Hemu with his own sacred hand," and to acquire merit by a holy combat."[1] Although loyalists pressed him, the boy Shahin Shah "showed himself more and more averse to the proceeding." Bairam khan, who had already made up his mind, when perceived that boy emperor was not inclined to take his view, withdrew from the attempt, himself became engaged in the acquisition of this fancied merit, and with his sword cleansed the world from the contamination of his existence. Hemu was thus executed.[2]

Al-Badaoni has also recorded that "...Shaikh Geda-i-Kamboh and others, said to the emperor — since this is your Majesty's first war against the infidels, you should flash your sword in this unbeliever for such an act would have great reward."

But the boy emperor replied — "why should I strike him now that he is already as good as dead? If sensation and activity were left in him, I would do so."[3]

Fredrick Augustus, Count of Noer also gives a similar version when he says:

"While the savage rout of fugitives and pursued raged to a greater and greater distance, Hemu, sorely wounded, was brought into the presence of Akbar who had joined Bairam Khan after the battle. The latter asked the emperor to strike off the prisoner's head and thus, by slaying an infidel win for himself the coveted title of *Ghazi* — (a champion, a hero, especially one who fights against infidels) — but the generous boy could not bring himself to kill a fallen and captive foe. To end the delay and to accustom his young sovereign to the sight of blood, Bairam Khan himself shorn off Hemu's head."[4]

Bairam Khan was followed by Gada-i-Shaikh, and others who were present there. Badaoni goes on to record — "Thus was fulfilled the saying — what is the good of killing one who is going to be burnt? — and they found this mine mosyuon for the date:-

If through treachery, deceit and fraud great Delhi fell,
By Fate's decree into the hands of Hindu Hemun;
Muhammad Akbar, that Shah whose glory reached the sky.
By help of God captured that black-faced Hindu Hemun,
Creator's scribe on lasting table with pen of power.
Wrote concerning that day; he seized Hindu Hemun'.[5]

The above mentioned stories regarding Akabar's refusal to severe the head of Hemu, dubbed by historians as official version, seemed to have been invented by "courtly flatterers". Vincent Smith has rightly commented, when he says. "...Akbar, a boy of 14 cannot be justly blamed for complying with the instructions of Bairam Khan, who had a right to expect obedience; nor is there any good reason for supposing that at that time the boy was more scrupulous than his officers. The official story, that a magnanimous sentiment of unwillingness to strike a helpless prisoner already half-dead compelled him to refuse to obey his guardians instructions, seems to be the late invention of courtly flatterers..."[6]

Statements of Ahmad Yadgar and the Dutch writer, Vanden Brocke, who derived his information from a 'Genuine chronicle of the Kingdom', also contradict the story. Vanden Brocke says, "The soldiers of Hemu ... ... deserting their leader, went off in various directions, so that the Mughals gained possession of all the baggage and the elephants, and Hemu, having been struck by an arrow in the eye during the fight, was constrained to fly; but, having been caught and brought back by Shah Quli Mahram-i-Baharbi was placed before Akbar, who had come up in a burry on hearing of the rout of the Pathans. Akbar, at the request of Ali Quli Khan by a deed unworthy of a prince, severed the neck of the surrendered prisoner with a scimitar, and directed the head to be affixed to the gate of Delhi."[7]

The description given by Ahmad Yadgar tallies to some extent with that of the Dutch writer but is widely different from the rest of the narratives. He says. "It chanced that, by decree of the Almighty, an arrow struck Hemun in the forehead. He told his elephant driver to take the elephant out of the field of battle ... ... When Shah Quli Beg was told of what had occurred he came upto the elephant, and brought it into the presence of Bairam Khan. Bairam Khan after prostrating himself and returning thanks caused Hemu to descend from the elephant, after which he bound his hands, and took him before the young and fortunate Prince and said — as this is our first success, let your Highness's own august hand smite this infidel with the sword. The Prince accordingly, struck him and divided his head from his unclean body.(Nov. 5 1556 A.D)"[8]

Jehangir, in his memoirs has also given an interesting account of the incident, he says, "A number of men immediately conveyed Hemu *as he was* to the King (Akbar). Bairam Khan represented that it would be proper if the King with his own hand should strike the infidel with a sword, so that by obtaining the reward of a *Ghazi* (warrior of the faith) he might use this title on the imperial farmans.

The boy king answered, "I have cut him in pieces before this", and explained: "One day, in Kabul, I was copying a picture in presence of Khwaja Abdul-Samad Shirin — Qalm, when a form appeared from my brush,the parts of which were separate and divided from each other. One of them near asked, whose picture is this? It came to my tongue to say that it was the likeness of Hemu — Not defiling his hand with his (Hemu's) blood, he told one of his servants to cut off his head..."[9]

The above mentioned version of the story, Jehangir must have heard from the people at the *durbar* and thus found occasion to incorporate the same in his Memoirs. As Vincent Smith has also remarked, that it was surprising that the account given by the Prince, the authenticity of which cannot be doubted differed from that of Abul Fazl. However there is no doubt that the most detailed description of what happened when Hemu was executed, is available only in *Akbarnama*. It is clearly mentioned by him that Hemu was unconscious and when questioned, made no reply. It is only conjecture that he was so overwhelmed by shame and indisposed to say anything. The fatal wound could not have kept him alive for so long.

According to Abul Fazl, Akbar regarded him lifeless, but the more the loyalists and courtier pressed him, the more averse he became. The Mughal chronicler, the erstwhile court historian has given the boy emperor, the credit for the decision, not to "stain the holy skirt of his mind with such dust, and if such an event occur, how shall he stain his sword with the blood of such a moribund, impure wretch." This is exactly a description which a flatterer and a courtier could record to please his master in medieval India of the sixteenth Century.

As Akbar at the time of Hemu's execution, was an unregenerate lad, devoted to amusement, cannot be credited with the feelings of his mature manhood.[10] He had not the courage to defy the orders of his tutor-guardian; and so struck the sword. Moreover the charm and attraction of assuming the title of *Ghazi* was too tempting to be resisted by the boy Emperor. This is confirmed by the hard fact that Akbar assumed the high sounding title of *Ghazi* from the very first year of the reign and used that in his *firmans*. This was naturally assumed due to his having slain his Hindu opponent, Hemu, *even though he was lifeless*. What a pity that the Mughal emperor, *Akbar the Great*, felt honoured throughout his life, *on having slain a dead man*.

Jehangir in his Memoirs has clearly hinted that Akbar was advised to do the above feline act for obtaining the title, so that the same could be used on the imperial *firmans* and paraded in the Islamic world. That Akbar, when grown up, prided in using: the title, shows that he had no qualms or any sense of guilt, but did so in obedience to the commands of his tutor-guardian. It is immaterial whether he struck the sword, or merely touched it, whilst over the neck of Hemu, the fact remains that the victim was as good as dead and his hands were bound.[11]

Conclusion :

The various narratives given above about the executions of Hemu, widely differ in many details, although minor. The main question undoubtedly resolves on one point, whether Akbar obeyed the tutor guardian or not? Whether he felt scruples at the time of complying with Bairam Khan's instructions, howsoever unpalatable? Or did he order any of the officers or his obedient courtier servants to perform the deed or he took the trouble himself.' Abul Fazl's rhetorical version, Badaoni's plain narrative, and corroborative statements of Faizee and Abdullah, author of *Tarikh-i-Daudi*, and categorically opposite versions of Ahmad Yadgar, Fredrick Augustus, Count of Noer as well as de Laet confound the reader today. Dispassionately studying the various accounts, considering the relatively immature age of Akbar and the circumstances under which he was being tutored as well as commanded lead one to the conclusion, that the following version of the incident's narrative recorded by Ferishta appears to be nearer to reality and truth.

"When Hemu was brought into the presence, Bairam Khan recommended to the King to do a meritorious act by killing the infidel with his own sword. Akbar in order to fulfil the wish of his minister, drew his sword, and *touching the head of the captive became entitled to the appellation of Ghazi* : while Bairam Khan, drawing his own sabre, at a single blow severed the head of Hemu from his body."[12]

After the severance of head from the body, Hemu's head was sent to Kabul, to give lesson to the superficial Afghans, who had the audacity to co-operate with him. According to Abul Fazl "the head of Hemu was brought and hung up on the iron gate of Kabul, the drums of joy beat high, and after thanksgiving and rejoicing," the expedition carrying the Mughal ladies set out for India. The trunk was conveyed to Delhi and reported to have been hung on gibbet as a warning to the future opponents of the Mughals. According to some chroniclers this martyrdom took place on 13th November 1556. But it does not seem to be quite correct, as the execution could not have been delayed so much. On the other hand the Mughals were so apprehensive, that they committed the foul deed hastily. They dare not keep Hemu, dead or unconscious, as a captive.

In case there was any life left in Hemu, the captive, humanity demanded that instead of being executed, he should have been given medical treatment and kept a war-prisoner for some time. Abul Fazl had hinted that they might have kept Hemu in prison and made him desirous of serving the threshhold of fortune. But in the medieval canons of justice brutality was no crime, humanity was taboo. But it is evident that no life was left in the body of Hemu and all the drama of execution was enacted to proclaim the boy emperor Akbar as GHAZI — the slayer of an infidel. This attitude was quite opposite to what, Akbar's grandfather Babur showed to his adversary, Sultan Ibrahim who lay dead in the field, amidst fifteen thousand of his dead. Babur lifted up the head of his dead adversary, and reported to have said, "Honour to your courage," ordered brocade and sweetmeats ready', "enjoined Dilawar Khan and Khalife to bathe the corpse and to bury it where it lay."[13]

Spoils of War :

The victorious Mughal soldiers, of the so-called divine army, marched towards Delhi, and indulged in indiscriminate slaughter of the fugitives. Their primary aim was collection of spoils. Sikandar Khan Uzbeg, who was entrusted with the task of pursuing the fleeing got immense booty. It was the common practice in those days, for the victors to loot the vanquished. Even women and children were not spared. At times they also became a part of the booty and were disposed off or sold as slaves. The casualties in the battle ran into thousands; and hundreds and thousands, who might have been trampled or harassed, their number was not known.

According to Al-Badaoni, on the second day after the victory, when Akbar, the boy emperor came to Panipat, he had a minaret built of the heads of the slain. From Panipat after the execution of Hemu, Akbar reached Delhi and caused the *Khutbah* to be proclaimed from the pulpit.[14] He stayed one month, and appointed the Mughal Amirs again as governors of Agra, Sambhal, and other towns.

Prior to the second battle of Panipat, Bairam Khan had persuaded boy emperor to seek the blessings of the famous Saint Shaikh Jalal. According to Ahmad Yadgar, "Bairam Khan took the prince into the presence of Kutbul Aktal Saiyad Jalal Thaneswari and procured, the honour of kissing the feet of that most holy individual. When they were about to depart, they begged him to give them the assistance of his prayers. They said 'This accused infidel is coming with an army numerous as ants and locusts, it is proper that your holiness should protect the cause of Islam — The Saiyed reflected for a short time, and then said to them, — Have you not heard what little boys at play say? — He then dismissed them". This clearly shows that Akbar and his tutor-guardian were quite diffident and were anxious to seek the blessings of a saint like the Shaikh for victory in the battle against Hemu.[15]

Location of the battle-field : G. Khurana has reexamined the issue. At Badaoni has mentioned a place named Kharmanda, which Hemu had reached after starting from Panipat.[16] Thereafter he came to the district of Kharmanda and fighting began beyond Panipat. According to Abul Fazl the place was Sarai Kaharunda Karunda.[17] Ahmad Yadgar, although does not name the place but mentions Hemu's seting his camp two *kos* west of Panipat. This has been corroborated by Vincent Smith in his book *Akbar* as well as in the *Karnal District Gazetter* (1910).

According to G. Khurana the battle-field extended from Sarai Pilkhan to Kharmanda and must have spread over an area of about two or five kos southwest of Panipat. On the basis of this the author concludes that Hemu might have camped his army in the vicinity of the Ferozshahi Canal (in the west of Panipat) which assured supply of water for his soldiers and their animals. So Kharmanda being situated on the eastern side of the canal, the battle must have been fought by Hemu around it on 5th November 1556 A.D.

Analysing the details of the battle of Panipat, given by Abul Fazl, Nizamuddin Ahmad and others it is evident that in the battle field, there was a great ravine which "even elephant could not cross."[18] The bands of archers under Ali Quli Khan Shaibani then did the yeamon service by compressing into a small space and standing firm, awaiting opportunity to attack. Accordingly they showed such endurance that the elephants retreated before the ouslaught of arrows and the centre became vulnerable. The arches streaked into the rear of Hemu's army also and discharged their arrows, in addition to wielding their swords. It is clear that the fierce and decisive battle took place near a ravine, which saved the Mughals from the frontal attack of the elephants of Hemu's army. *Dalpat Vilas,* a Rajasthan work also mention the crossing of a nullah by the Mughal army on the eve of the battle.[19]

Nirod Bhushan Roy has rightly commented, "victory attended his army everywhere and his military fame spread. Hero of two and twenty battles, victorious against formidable opponents like Taj Khan, Ibrahim Khan, Muhammad Shan and Tardi Beg Khan, his very name caused a shudder in the Mughal army. His influence over soldiers was unbounded."[20] In actuality Hemu's defeat at Panipat was accidental and Akbar's victory Providential.

Note and References

1. *Akbarnama.,* Vol.II. p.65.
2. Ibid. Shaikh Gadai, the *sadr,* a favourite of Bairam Khan followed suit, he was appointed to *sadarat,* replacing Maulana Abdual Baqi in that capacity.

3. *Muntakhabu-T-Tawarikh.*, Vol.II. pp.9-12.
4. *The Emperor Akbar*, Vol.II., p.72.
5. *Muntakhabu-T-Tawarikh*, Vol.II. p.9
6. *Akbar the Great Mugul.*, p. 39
7. *Journal of Royal Asiatic Society*: 1916 pp. 527-555 The Death of Hemu fn. *De Laet, De Imperio Magni Sive India Vera*, Lugduni Bataverma, Elzevir, 1631., p.174-181. There are two issues, with a different paging, both bearing the date 1631. The passage is from the *Fragmentum Historic Indicae* by Van den Brocke. (Eng. Trs. by Smith — De Laet has translated from the Dutch of Vander Broacke.) According to *Akbarnama*, p.85, the head was affixed to the iron gate of Kabul and not Delhi.
8. Ahmad Yadgar. *Tarikh-i-Salatin — Afghana* — Elliot and Dowson, Vol-v. pp.65-66.
9. *Jehangir-Nama*, (Eng. Trs.) — by Alexander Rogers, ed. by Henry Beveridge p.40.
10. Vincent Smith; *Akbar the Great Mugal.*, p.39 and the *fn*.
11. A painting of Hemu, hands bound in the back, is said to be in the National Museum, at Dublin Ireland.
12. *The Rise of the Mahomedan Power*, (trs. Briggs.) Vol.II. pp.184-190.
13. Lane-poole., *Babar.*, p.164 and Elliot and Dowson, Vol.v. pp.29-30.
14. *Muntakhabu-T-Tawarikh.*, Vol. II. p.10.
15. Haryana: *Ancient and Medieval*, pp. 140-141 quoted *Tarikh-i-Salatin-i-Afghana*: also the *Bibilo Theca Indica* text of the *Tarikh-Mubarakshahi.*
16. Proceedings of the Panjab History Conference, 1978, pp.68-70: *Muntakhab-at-Tawarikh*, Eng.trans.Vol. II. p.8.
17. *Akbarnama*, Vol.II. p.54: according to *Ain-i-Akabari*, Vol. II. the place has been identified as kharkbud. The place is called Serai Kharunda in the *Khulasal-Tawarikh*. The correct name appears to he Kharmanda.
18. *Akbarnama*, vol.II. p.64.
19. Ravat Sarswat, Sadul Rajasthan Resarch Institute Bikaner, 1960, pp.8-20. The Successors of Sher Shah, pp.88-89.
20. *The Successors of Sher Shah*, pp. 88-89.

[illegible] Vol. II, p. 12.

[illegible] Vol. II, p. 272.

[illegible] Vol. II, p. [illegible]

[illegible] p. 93.

[illegible]

[illegible] the National [illegible]

[illegible]

CHAPTER-IX

The Aftermath

According to Al-Badaoni besides the elephants, "... treasure and stores, to such an amount that even fancy is powerless to imagine it, were taken as spoil." Among these who pursued the fugitives, the chief were Pir Muhammad Khan, and many others, in consort with Sa'id Khan, the Moghul. While passing "from Alwar they came up to the wife of Hemu, who had with her elephants laden with gold."[1]

Abul fazl has also mentioned that before the first year of Akbar's reign came to a close, i.e. January 1557, A.D., Pir Muhammad Khan "took possession of the Sarkar of Alwar as far as Deoli Sajari (or Sachari), the birth place of Hemu."[2] Deoli was fortified by nature and fit for putting up a resolute defence. So no wonder that when the Mughal forces reached the place, Hemu's father resisted them and was captured after a fight.

Execution of Hemu's father :

Rai Purandas, Hemu's saintly father, who was eighty years old, was arrested and brought before Maulana Pir Muhammad Khan. According to Al-Badaoni he was originally Mulla, and having become closer and opener of every important affair of State, and finance, as Viceregent of the Khan-Khanan, assumed airs of an Amir. When he confronted Rai Purandas, he asked him to change his religion and accept Islam or meet the punishment of death. To this the octogenarian saint replied with all composure, "For eighty years. I have worshipped my God, according to my religion, why should I change it now at the sunset of my life and that too merely for fear of life, and without understanding how it disturbs you in your worship."

Pir Muhammad, fanatic as he was, paid no heed to such a dignified reply and got the old saintly father of Hemu executed forthwith. In the words of Abul Fazl, "he was killed by him. After gathering his spoils, Pir Muhammad returned to Akbar."[3] Pir Muhammad Khan, Bairam Khan's personal *wakil*, became a key figure in the administration.

Escape of Hemu's Wife :

Al Badaoni has graphically mentioned that the vast treasure collected by Hemu for the conduct of incessant wars, feeding the army and its animals, was under the care of his wife. Her elephants were laden with gold. As soon as she learnt of the Mughals following her, "she herself gained the mountain and jungle ground in the district of Kuwa and Baijwara but left the gold behind, the greater part of which the rustics of the country of Baijwara seized; still the part which fell into the army of the faithful was so great that they gave it... away by shieldfulls and "nizar-i-Zarha" — Scattering of gold pieces — was found to give the date (964)." The place has not been identified, but it could not be in the Punjab, in the neighbourhood of the river Sutlej as mentioned by Lowe, nor in the present Haryana. Had she done so, she would have been captured easily, so Lowe's footnote, on p. 10, *Akbarnama*, Vol. II. is incorrect. Similarly Jarett's identification of Baijwara in the Sarkar of Agra also does not stand scrutiny. However it has been revealed that she fled to a place where her parents lived. This was a place in present day Rajasthan, identified as Bhadkol in Arawali hills by Dr. Manhar Gopal.

Badaoni has further recorded that "And on the road, which the Queen took, there had fallen such quantities of coins and ingots of gold, that for many a year traveller and passers-by used to find them. In this measure the treasures, which Sher Shah and Aslim Shah, and Adali had amassed through a course of years, were dissipated".[4]

The verses that have been added after that clearly show the prejudices with which Badaoni recorded them. They smell like a sermon to the vauquished. The chronicler had forgotten, when he wrote that the treasure, of the Sur's was given by Adli to Hemu to organise expeditions against his Afghan rivals and Humayun. It passes one's comprehension how any general could fight twenty-two battles without ample finances. Hemu was no doubt ablest minister of Islam Shah who could manage civil as well as military affairs. So he took over the entire treasure from the forts, fought the battles and had at his disposal enough to run the administration. But for the accidental defeat in the battle of Panipat he might have managed the throne of Delhi ably. There was no question of his seizing the treasure as spoil; he never took that for his self, but he acquired that for fighting the battles and maintaining the armies to restore law and order. Had he kept the hoarded treasure in forts of Chunar, Rohtas or Gwalior he would not been able to maintain and win laurels with such huge armies, which Abul Fazl and Badaoni, both have praised. The problem before him was not only to feed the soldiers, but also the army animals, whose consumption of cereals was staggering.

Prof. Satish Chandra in one of his articles on Hemu has commented that Hemu at the time of his death was a rich man. Needless to say that the Sircar of Alwar was one of the richest and except for a short period between the first battle of Panipat and Humayun's flight from India, Alwar, Mahendargarh (Kanaud), Rewari area was a prosperous area. And Hemu's parents living in Macheri, Alwar, and then Rewari were from well to-do family, having landed property in Qutubpur (Rewari). It is also known from his community members that, whilst as a minister of Islam Shah, Hemu built his own palatial house on a hillock in the present Jama Masjid area. It was during Islam Shah's time that on the other hillock Salimgarh was built. This must have been an open area, as Old Delhi at that time was located somewhere near Tughluqabad and Haus Khas. As Akbar preferred to make Agra his capital, so this area and the house built by Hemu for his residence must have fallen into ruins. It was only in Shah

Jahan's time that these two rocky areas were selected for the construction of the Red Fort and Jama Masjid. The later hillock was known as Bhojla Pahari.

Flight of Haji Khan : Having disposed of Hemu's saintly father and having failed to check the escape of Hemu's wife with vast treasure, the Mughals chased Haji Khan, who was acting a Governor of Mewat. He had already distinguished himself for prudence, and helped in the mobilization of Hemu's army. It was his last minute attack that won for Hemu the battle of Delhi and led to the rout of the Mughals. As the time of the battle of Panipat, in all probability he was in Mewat, guarding the vast treasure. But after the disaster at Panipat and the accidental death of Hemu, Haji Khan felt, "frightened by the strength of the victorious (Mughal) army and fled before its arrival."[5]

As a result of Haji Khan's flight, the whole of the Sarkar of Mewat, came into the possession of the Mughals. Haji Khan driven away by the Mughals moved towards south-west, and found refuge at Ajmer, where he was attacked by Maldev as he had plundered a few villages of Marwar. He appealed for help to Uday Singh, who immediately responded and rescued Haji Khan. Rana Uday Singh was assisted by Rao Surjan Singh Hada of Bundi and Rao Jaimal of Mirtha etc. Even Ruler of Bikaner Kalyanwal joined Haji Khan. Marwar forces withdrew this time. The Rana then demanded his price. He desired the surrender of a favourite mistress of the Afghan general, which he refused. He was also asked to give forty maunds of gold. Having refused both the things Haji Khan made a bold stand against the Rana with his few thousand followers. A battle took place on January 24, 1557 A.D. in which Rana was defeated. Haji Khan secured the assistance of Raja Maldeo of Marwar and Muzaffar Khan Sarwani also came to his help. With their help Haji Khan succeeded in capturing Ajmer, Nagor and adjoining territories. Haji Khan retained Ajmer and Maldeo was satisfied with Mirtha.

The Mughals and Haji Khan : In December 1557 A.D. Akbar was at Lahore and there felt unhappy as Bairam Khan, aged fifty at that time, married Salima, a cousin of Akbar, but only nineteen years old. However he decided to move from Lahore to Delhi via

Jalandar. After crossing the Sutlej, he learnt of the growing power of Haji Khan Mewati, who had by that time subdued Ajmer-Merwara, and was threatening Hissar too. Bairam Khan was asked to send reinforcements immediately under Pir Muhammad. Haji Khan managed to escape to Gujarat. He was also joined there by Haji Khan Basawani, who had figured prominently in negotiations between the Mughals and Sangram Khan, who also fled to Gujarat and joined Haji Khan.[6]

The Mughals thereafter took possession of Ajmer and adjoining territories. Akbar returned to Delhi on April 14, 1558 A.D. Haji Khan Mewati was reported to have withdrawn first towards Marwar and ultimately to Gujarat. Mewat, which was at one time conferred as Jagir on Tardi Beg Khan, was then given to Pir Muhammad, for his good services.

Pursuit of Sikundur Sur : While Hemu was entrenched in the throne of Delhi, and the Mughals were desperately trying to extirpate him, Khizr Khwaja had been appointed to oppose Sikundur Sur, who was threatening them from the Siwalik hills. As there was no concerted action between Hemu and Sekundur Sur, the Mughals could concentrate on fighting one after the another. When *khutba* was read in Delhi in the name of Akbar...." news came to Delhi, that on the confines of chamyari, a place with 20 *cosses* of Lahore, Khizr Khan had been defeated before Sikundur, and had arrived at Lahore."[7] When the Mughal forces departed for Jalandhar, Sikundur again hid himself in the mountains of Siwalik; and the Mughal forces had to penetrate upto Dahmiri. Sikundur shut himself up in the fortress of Mankot, and the Mughals continued to attack him day by day. The seige lasted for six months.

In the meantime Mulla Abdullah Sultanpuri played a dual role. On the one hand he received from the Afghans the title of Shaikh-al-Islam and from the Mughals that of Makhdumul-mulk.[8] However due to the perseverence of Muhammad Hasayn Khan, and his brother Hasan Beg, who was killed, the seige turned out of long duration. Being deserted by his followers, Sikundur sent peace proposals. Sayyid Mahmud Barha along with Ghazi Khan Sur, came to Akbar with a present of elephants, and through the intervention of Atka Khan and Pir Muhammad Khan, surrendered the fort on 25th Ramjan in the year 964, July 1557 A.D. i.e. 24th May 1557. Akbar agreed to grant the fief of Jaunpur to Sikundur, as soon as that could be conquered by Khan Zaman from the Afghans. The charge of the seige of the fort of Mankot was made over by Akbar to the Khan Khanam and he joined the Mughal ladies and indulged in mutual rejoicings. The Mughal army which had become straightened by the long siege were greatly rejoiced. The conquest of this fort was regarded as of prime importance. Arrangements for the siege were excellently laid and carried out, and the entrenchments were pushed forward on all sides. Though Sikandar relied on the strength of the fort but he was disheartened by the appearance of affairs.

Abul Fazl had also mentioned that the Afghans were calculating that Mubariz Khan Adli, who was all the time in Chunar fort when Hemu crowned himself at Delhi and fought the battle of Panipat, "... would be able to lift up his head from the eastern provinces of India and march against Delhi, and so the siege of the fort (Mankot) would not be completed, and that so her (Sikunder) would be able to get an opportunity for commotion in the tranquillised districts, he did not give up defending the fort, "But in 1557 A.D. Sikundar thought it right to compromise by surrendering the fort and earning forgiveness. He was allowed to go to the East — *Kharid* and Bihar. After two years he went to the abode of annihilation.[9]

End of Mubariz Khan Adli :

During this period, when Akbar was fighting against Sikundar Sur, the ruler of Bengal, Sadr Khan (also called Khizr Khan Sur), the son of Muhammad Khan took upon himself the title of Jalalu-d-din and made great pretentions. According to Abul Fazl he in order to avenge the death of his father, whom Mubariz Khan had slain in the battle of Chunar (Monghyr according to Steward) killed him in the battle. A great battle ensued in which Mubariz Khan was killed in 1557 A.D. Thus died two of the Sur claimants to the throne of Delhi, and the third one, viz. Ibrahim

Sur took refuge in Orissa, where he met his doom about ten years later. (1567-1568) A.D. In this way Hemu's death sounded the death knell of the hegemony of the Surs — The Pathans as well.

Plight of Sikandar Sur : According to Abul Fazl when Sikandar witnessed rising fortune of the Mughals and his own defeats after defeat, despair upon despair fell upon. He decided to seek forgiveness and sent his son as a slave. He is also alleged to have won the heart of the Mughal ambassador "by deceitful blandishments and submissions," and also sent presents in money and goods to the Nasir-ul-Mulk, who was the Khan-Khanan's vakil, or rather was the *vakil* of the Sultanate..."[10]

Akbar assigned to Sikandar *Kharid* and Bihar as Jagirs. Sikandar surrendered the fort of Mankot and departed for the East. After two years, i.e. in 1559 A.D. he died. By 7 December 1557 the Mughal armies could move towards the capital of Delhi. The Government of Lahore was entrusted by Akbar to Husain Khan's, sister's son of Mahdi Qasim Khan, Bairam Khan heaved a sign of relief and, while the army was encamped at Jalandhar, he married Salima Sultan Begum. The marriage and the bridal procession took place within one week. Salima, who was distinguished for good qualities, was only nineteen years old and Bairam Khan had attained the age of over fifty. As mentioned by several historians Akbar wanted to marry her, but Humayun had already destined Salima for Bairam Khan, so the latter hastened to marry her. Consequently "soon after the estrangement commenced between Akbar and him." After the death of Bairam Khan Akbar married her in 968 A.H.[11]

During this period the Mughals took resort to diplomacy and began to buy off Afghan's defiance by wooing them. The followers of Sikandar Sur had deserted him one by one and joined the Mughal court. Sayyid Mahmud Barha along with Ghazi Khan Sur, had come to the boy emperor Akbar and presented elephants on 22nd *Ramzan* 964, corresponding to 1558 A.D. How Sikandar Sur was forced to surrender had already been detailed.:

Battle of East : Khan Zaman advanced towards Lucknow (Oudh) and Jaunpur to subdue the the recalcitrant Afghans. He was opposed by Hasan Khan Bachgoti with 20,000 men; but Khan Zaman and Bahadur Khan, succeeded in defeating the Afghans at Lucknow. The next engagement took place at Jaunpur with the Bengali Afghan, who called himself Sultan Bahadur and had issued coin and caused the *Khutba* to be read in his name in Bengal. The victory at Jaunpur was of great importance, "as it reopened the eastern provinces to the Mughals. Large booty and huge stores fell into the hands of the victor, Khan Zaman who was then equipped for further exploits..."[12] According to Abul Fazl he acquired "immense fortune by plunder."[13]

Gwalior : Upto the years 966 A.H. i.e. 1558 A.D., Gwalior continued to be held by the Afghans under Bubail Khan (Bhil Khan) a *ghulam* of Adli and Hemu. The Mughal forces besieged him, and forced him to sue for quarter and hand over the keys. The fort of Gwalior was one of the famous fortresses of India and had few like it for strength. Raja Ram Sah tried to capture the fort, but the Mughal under Qiya Khan gave him battle and defeated him at Agra. Thereafter he besieged the fort of Gwalior.[14]

Ranthombhor : One of the most important forts of Rajasthan continued to be held by Sangram Khan, a slave of Adli and Hemu. But in 1558 A.D., scenting danger of its capture by the Mughals, he sold that to Rai Surjan Hada. Prior to that he had struggled hard to fight against Hindu Beg, but due to the intervention by Haji Khan Bhikan, Basawari and Al-Badaoni's father, but failing to get success, he sued for peace. But when the Mughal Amirs practised delay and procrastination in the payment of compensation in ready money and goods, Sangram Khan handed the fort to the Rajputs. Sangram Khan along with Haji Khan, a trusted general of Hemu migrated to Gujarat to escape the wrath of the Mughals.

Acquisition of Chunar : The strong fort of Chunar, the seat of Adli's government in the East, continued to be held by Jamal Khan, a slave of Adli. When he heard of the approach of Khan Zaman, the Mughals sent Mehar Ali Beg to treat with. He carried a *firman* containing terms.[15] Jamal received the messenger with great cordiality, and showed him the palaces of Sher Shah and Salim Shah, as well as all the munitious stored in the fort. But when the *firman* of conciliation containing a grant of five parganas in Jaunpur was shown to Jamal Khan, he was disillusioned, as he pitched his expectations higher.

Consequently in reply to the above-mentioned terms, he proposed his own terms to Mhir Ali. He also attempted to detain him till an answer to his representation came from the Mughal court. In the meantime his negtotiations with Khan Zaman, and Fath Khan Afghan, who was at the fortres of Rohtas, bore fruit. Mhir Ali scented treachery and was alarmed due to the expected defection of Fath Khan and insubordination of Khan Zaman.

He tried to escape, by running from the fort of Chunar, unattended across the Ganges, in the greatest perturbation. Having failed in his mission Mhir Ali returned to Agra. The fortress of Chunar was left in the hands of Jamal Khan.[16]

Sometime after, the fortress of Chunar was again commanded by another Afghan slave of Adli. He was assisted by Fattu and Sher Khan, son of Adli. They had a large army and 500 elephants.[17] Although Khan Zaman had gained a victory against them at Jaunpur, Fattu's fame had already spread all-round. He also sent a petition to the Mughal court offering to surrender the fort. In order to deal with him, Shaikh Muhammad (of whom Fattu was a devoted disciple), and Asaf Khan went and took peaceful possession of the fortress of Chunar. Fattu, mentioned by Al-Badaoni as Masuadi Al-Fattu, a slave of Adli, entered Mughal service, and later on served them well.[18]

Fall of Bairam Khan : During the first five years Bairam Khan was given all respect and honour, but when Akbar discovered his sedition, he issued a *firman* detailing the circumstances that led to the removal of the prime-minister, the *vakil*. He was given full freedom to govern and nourish the family of the boy emperor; accordingly, "whatever he wished, good or bad, was carried out, and thus in these five years some improper acts of his came to light which disgusted everyone, such as his patronage of Sheikh Gadai...."[19]

Exception was taken to Bairam Khan's "private companionship and intimacy" with him, and his making him Sadr and allowing him to "endorse decrees with his seal...." He also exempted him from the ceremony of doing homage (*taslim*). Besides that Bairam Khan gave to his menial servants the titles of Sultan and Khan, and presented them with flags, kettle-drumms, rich fief, and productive terriories. On the other hand he reduced the existing Amirs, the officers to want of even dry bread.

In short Bairam Khan was charged with having committed "various immoderate and disproportionate acts." He also practiced various kinds of oppression and insults for purposes of espial. He believed his flatterers more than the true-speakers. When his faults were made known to him, he utterly forgot the favour shown to him. The *firman* has recorded that as the boy emperor "wished to please him as a sincere well-wisher of our family, and fully relied upon his words and action,..." he passed over his actions and faults, with consummate benevolence.

But at last when it was reported to Akbar that Bairam Khan meditated rebellion, by separating the well-wishers and reducing the boy emperor to solitude, then he proceeded from Agra to Delhi to defeat his wickedness. Even then he was given opportunity to retract and not defame his name for rebellion, contumacy and sedition. Bairam Khan's treatment of Pir Muhammad Khan, while retreating to Gujarat annoyed Akbar and accelerated Bairam Khan's fall.

When Bairam Khan went on from the Pargana of Bikaner to the Punjab, near the fort of Tabarhinda, he was given battle near Tharah. His son Abdur Rahim and family, who were left in the fort, were escorted to the Mughal court. Wali Beg came to Tharah and was defeated. He went to Jalandhar. Thereafter Bairam Khan fell from royal favour and wherever he went, he suffered a loss. Bairam Khan's place was taken by Munim Khan, who was appointed as *vakil* and styled Khan-Khanan. His influence had been increasing ever since the arrival of Mughal ladies from Kabul, and the marriage of the king to the daughter of Mirza Abdulla Mughal, a son-in-law of Munim Khan.

Bairam Khan scuttles : From the wording of the *firman* it would appear that Akbar was all the time very conciliatory and respectful to his guardian tutor. But Bairam Khan was precipate and took hasty steps. When he heard that Akbar had assumed the reins of Government, he left Agra under the pretext of going to Mecca via Meerut and Nagor. But from there, as a mark of protest, he returned his insignia, which reached Akbar at Jhujhar. Akbar naturally moved to Punjab, where Bairam Khan was expected to raise the standard of revolt.

When Pir Muhammad heard of Bairam Khan's disgrace, he at once returned to Akbar from Gujarat, and was made a Khan. Akbar, in order to counteract Bairam Khan's seditious move, conferred the *insignia* on Pir Muhammad Khan, Bairam Khan's old *protege*, who was ordered to see him off to Mecca. Bairam Khan felt infuriated at that. He could not go to Gujarat as Raja Maldev, his enemy blocked the way; so he proceeded to Bikaner to his friend Kalyan Mal.[20]

Acting desperately Bairam Khan revolted, fight took place at Dipalpur and Jalandhar and the Mughal forces under Atgah Khan defeated him. Bairam Khan was reported to have fled to the fort Tilwara on the banks of Beas (Punjab) followed by Akbar. Fighting again ensued, and casualties took place. Bairam Khan accompanied by the principal grandees, went to Akbar's tent, and was pardoned.

After staying for two days longer, with Munim Khan, he received a sum of money and was sent to Mecca. Haji Muhammad of Sistan accompanied Bairam Khan over Nagor to Patan (Nabrwala) in Gujarat where he was received by Musa Khan Fuladi, the governor. Bairam Khan's following among the nobles built so labouriously during the preceding five years melted away. Even some of his trusted lieutenants either deserted him or adopted an attitude of neutrality.

Killed at Patan : According to reliable sources, on Friday, 14th Jumada I, 968 A.H. (1561 A.D.), While alighting from boat after a trip to Sahansa Lang tank, Bairam Khan was stabbed by a Lohani Afghan of the name of Mubarak Khan Lohani, whose father had been killed in the battle of Machhiwara. The Afghans were also unhappy because the Kashimiri wife of Salim Shah, with her daughter, was attached to Bairam Khan's suit going to Mecca, as he had agreed to betrothe his son to her. After his murder, some beggars lifted up his body and took that to the tomb of Shaykh

Husain'I-din. Akbar took charge of Bairam's infant son, Abdur Rahim, and married Salima Begum soon after, although Bairam's widow.[21]

Seventeen years later the body of Bairam Khan was interred in holy ground at Marh, had. Akbar had taken charge of Abdur-Rahim, Bairam's son. The child and his mother were brought by Muhammad Amir Diwane and Baba Zambur, from the scene of plunder to Ahmadabad "fighting the roads with the Afghan robbers."[22]

Death of Pir Muhammad Khan : Although Pir Muhammad was attached to Bairam Khan even in Qandahar, but when he had annoyed him, he retired him and forced to go on a pilgrimage. After Bairam Khan's death he again won Akbar's favour and defeated Baz Bahadur, who had invaded Malwa. He then made a raid into Khandesh, which was governed by Miram Muhammad Shah, sacked the capital Burhanpur, slaughtered most mercilessly the inhabitants, and carried off immense booty, when he was attacked by Baz Bahadur and defeated. Arriving at night on his flight at the bank of the Narmuda, he insisted on crossing it, and perished in the river.

Thus ended the two great iconoclasts, Bairam Khan and Maulana Pir Muhammad. By 1561-1562 Akbar was free from such influences, and he became more and more tolerant as well as receptive to the influence of saints and faqirs.[23]

Religious views of Akbar : Much has been written on the subject ever since the time of Badaoni and Abul Fazl, who are no doubt the best sources. H. Blochman, the translator of Abul Fazl's *Ain-i-Akbari* has written an illuminating note on that. Besides the two sources, Blochman has drawn special attention to the historical work entitled *Muntakhabu-T-Tawarikh,* written by an enemy of Akbar, whose character, in its grandeur and its failings,is much more prominent than in *Akbar-nama* or the *Tabaqat-i-Akbari* or the *Maasir-i-Rahim.* According to the translator's note it is especially of value for the religious views of the emperor, and contains interesting biographies of most famous men and poets of Akbar's time. The work was kept a secret and was made public during the reign of Jahangir, who showed his displeasure by disbelieving the statement of Badaoni's children that they themselves had been unaware of the existence of the book. The history ends with the beginning of 1004 A.H. or eleven years before Akbar's death in 1605 A.D. in 1594 A.D.; in all probability Badaoni died soon after.

Blochman had quoted an extract from Badaoni's work. According to Badaoni, during the years 986 A.H. i.e. 1583 A.D. many places of worship were built by the command of Akbar. The main cause of that was that by that date the Mughal emperor had gained in succession remarkable and decisive victories. All opponents had been eliminated and the empire had grown in extent. In the word of Badaoni, "His Majesty had thus leisure to come into nearer contact with ascetics and the disciples of the Musimiyyah sect and passed much of his time in discussing the word of God (Quran) and the word of he prophet (the Hudis, or Tradition). Questions of Sufism, scientific discussions, inquiries into philosophy and law, were the order of the day. His Majesty passed whole nights in thoughts of God; he continually occupied himself with pronouncing the names of *Ya Hu* (God) and *Ya Hadi* (God), which had been mentioned to him, and his heart was full of reverence for Him, who is the true Giver. From a feeling of thankfulness for his past successes, he would sit many a morning *alone* in prayer and malancholy, on a large flat stone of an old building, which lay near the palace in a lonely spot, with his head bent over his chest, and gathering the bliss of early hours."[24]

Badaoni has mentioned 983 A.H. as the date of the commencement of the Disputations, but he had not specified, whence he used to visit asceties and passed whole nights in thoughts of God. Lawrence Binyan's account based on Jesuit sources, assigns 563 A.D. or so as the date of the commencement of such trance.

Notes and References

1. *Muntakhabu-T-Tawarikh.*, Vol. II., pp. 9-10.
2. *Akbarnama*, Vol. II. pp. 71-72, According to District Gazetteer

of Alwar, Deoti and Macheri (Now in Rajgarh sub-division of Alwar District) had strongly defended forts, where Hemu's wife and his father had taken shelter with their precious goods and treasures.

3. *Ain-i-Akbari*, p. 387 and 387 fn. 1.
4. *Muntakhabu-T-Tawarikh.*, Vol. II. pp. 9-10; also *Akbar the Great*, by Dr. A.L. Srivastava, p. 30.
5. *Akbarnama*, Vol. II. pp. 71-72.
6. Ibid. Also, Gazetteer of Alwar, pp. 54-56.
7. *Muntakhabu-T-Tawarikh.*, Vol. II. p. 10.
8. *Akbarnama.*, Vol. II. p. 73 also *The Rise of the Mahomedan Power in India*, Vol. II. (Ferishta). pp. 190-191.
9. Ibid. pp. 89-91 : cf. *Sher Shah and his successors* by Nirod Bhushan Roy, pp. 91-96; also *Ain-i-Akbari* pp. 394-395. fn. 1.
10. Ibid., p. 90.
11. *Ain-i-Akbari*, pp. 321-322 and pp. 330-331.
12. *Muntakhabu-T-Tawarikh.*, Vol. II. pp. 18-19.
13. *Ain-i-Akbari.*, pp. 334-335. Also N. Roy's *Sher Shah and his successors*, pp. 91-96.
14. *Akbarnama.*, Vol. II. p. 68 : also N. Roy, *Sher Shah and his successors*, pp. 92-96.
15. *Muntakhabu-T-Tawarikh.*, Vol. II. pp. 26-27.
16. Ibid., pp. 42-44.
17. Ibid., pp. 42-44. also *Ain-i-Akbari*, p. 336.
18. Ibid., pp. 79-89.
19. *Akbarnama.*, Vol. II. pp. 161-176, the *Firman*, also *Ain-i-Akbari*, p. 342.
20. *Ain-i-Akbari.*, pp. 331-332 (No. 93) also *Medieval India* A Miscellany Aligarh, 1969. The Mughal Court politics during Bairam Khan's Regency.
21. Ibid., pp. 330-332 also *Akbarnama*, Vol. I. pp. 381-382.
22. Ibid., p. 355.
23. Ibid., p. 343; also Sri Ram Sharma, *Religious Policy of the Mughal emperors.*
24. Ibid. pp. 76-179. also *Jahangir-nama*, trs. by Alexander Rogers, ed. H. Beveridge, p. 38.

CHAPTER-X

Reconciliation

It is evident from the *firman* detailing the causes of termination of Bairam Khan's tutelage that Akbar allowed the Khan-i-Khanan and Maulana Pir Muhammad fullest freedom to deal with his adversaries, specially Hemu, his saintly father and his community members. The boy emperor might have been kind, humane and conciliatory, but till 1561 A.D. he had no opportunity to take his own decisions. However it has been asserted that as early as 1561, Akbar has started moving amongst the ascetics and faqirs near about Agra.

Dr. R.P. Tripathi has pointed out that in 1561, i.e. within five years of his accession and the execution of Hemu, Akbar had started moving incognito in the streets of Agra among the people, ascetics and *faqirs*.[1]

Akbar deliberately decided to follow a policy of understanding with the Afghans, the Hindus — particularly the Rajputs. In 968 A.H. i.e. 1562 A.D. Akbar married the daughter of Raja Bihari Mal and sister of Raja Bhagwan Das at Sambhar (Sabhar). it has been pointed to that when Humayun was fleeing from India to Persia, Bihari Mal a prince of Kachhwaha house, and a chief of Amber (Jaipur) had helped the Mughals, and the Governor of Narnaul, Majnum Khan Qaqshal in the retreat.

Akbar set his face against a militant and orthodox Islam. In 1563 he travelled to Mathura and Brindaban, and decided to abolish pilgrim taxes at Mathura. Next year he abolished the *zaziya*, the tax on the infidels, which brought in several crores of *dams*. Edicts to that effect were sent over the whole empire.

According to *Ain-i-Akbari* these orders were issued in 987 A.H. i.e. 1580 A.D. in that year he also made a pilgrimage to Ajmer. At a distance of five kos from the town, Akbar alighted and went on foot to the tomb of the Saint, Muinuddin Chishti. According to Abul Fazl, Akbar determined thereafter (1587 A.D.) to publicly use the formula — "There is no God, but God, and Akbar is God's representative."

Blochman further quoting from Badaoni, points out that, "His Majesty, from his *youth*, had also been accustomed to celebrate the *Hom* (a kind of fire-worship) from his affection towards the Hindu princesses of his Harem." Akbar according to Badaoni also was led to believe that it was wrong to kill cows, which the Hindus worshipped. he looked upon and killed beautiful mew instead of cows. The doctor confirmed the emperor in his opinion and told him it was written in their books that beef was productive of all sorts of diseases and was very indigestible.[2]

It has been further recorded by Badaoni that from the New Year's day of the twenty-fifth year of his reign, 988 A.H. — (1581 A.D.) Akbar openly worshipped the sun and the fire by prostrations; and the courtiers were ordered to rise when the candles and lamps were lighted in the palace. "On the festival of the eighth day of Virgo, *he put on the mark on the forehead,* like a Hindu, appeared in the Audience Hall, when several Brahmins tied, by way of auspiciousness, a string with jewels on it, round his hands, whilst the grandees countenanced these proceeding by bringing according to their circumstance, pearls and jewels as present. The custom of *Rakhi* (or tying pieces of cloth round the wrists as amulet) became quite common"

Badaoni has ascribed the changes in Akbar's attitude to the numerous Hindu princesses of the Harem, who had gained enormous influence over him. Not only had he forsworn beef, garlic, onions, but also wearing of a beard. He also introduced Hindu customs in the court to win the Hindus and their castes. He used to wear the Hindu mark on his forehead, and ordered sun worship four times a day. He himself prayed four times in twenty-four hours: at Sunrise, at noon, at sunset; and at midnight. He hardly slept for three hours. His day was full and a long one.

Most of such facts we know from Akbar's own historian, Abul Fazl, who was indeed fulsome in flattery, though he records with equanimity his acts. Lawrence Binyan has drawn attention to the accounts left by the Jesuits from Portugal. They had no motive for giving Akbar more than his due. In the words of Bartoli, Akbar "never gave anybody the chance to understand rightly his inmost sentiments or to know what faith or religion he held by ..."He was humane to even his enemy or traitor. According to Jesuit Father Monserrate, who accompanied Akbar on his Kabul expedition, Akbar was "by nature simple and straight forward." According to Lawrence Binyan he was in continual danger from his boyhood, he was surrounded by "treachery, jealousy, and intrigue." Akbar's clemency was proverbial, ever since his earlier years. He was prepared to take risks, and if those risked his life. That was why he, although more than a boy decided to marry a Hindu princess, in 1562. In the words of Binyan, "Such a marriage was a symbol of his irrevocable union with India and her destinies." He was born in India and identified himself with Hindus; the subtle influences of this matrimonial alliance was fruitful of consequences. He was experiencing spiritual wrestlings within himself, which were hidden from the world in early years. But people saw in his acts proof of that. He was imbued with the spirit of reconciliation, with Hindus with the family members and community people related to Hemu, Akbar's, greatest adversary. His good qualities, in the words of his son, Jahangir, were "beyond the limit of approval and the bounds of praise."[3]

Conciliatory measures : In 1563 Akbar was in camp at Mathura, presumably hunting tiger, when he learnt that the pilgrims to the holy places like Mathura and Brindaban were subjected to a levy of pilgrim tax, which brought revenue of million of rupees, he was indignant. He asserted that people gathered to worship throughout the Mughal empire. According to Lawrence Binyan, Akbar was so exhilarated by this merciful act, that he started on *padyatra* from Mathura to Agra, thirty-six miles stretch in a day. Of all his followers only an exhausted three arrived with him at Agra. He outstripped his court in body, how much more in mind.

Following the above conciliatory act, Akbar next year, in the same mood of generous impulse, decided to abolish *zaziya* — a tax levied on all dult males who were not Muslims. In Binyan's words, "It was an assertion of Akbar's will and conscience against a tradition of all the Muslim conquerors of India, sanctioned centuries of custom, against all his advisers, against the desire of his mother and his family. In a young man of twenty-two these acts astonish."[4] In short he was a born man of action, wise, tolerant, generous, capable of seeing far beyond his own time, and carrying his thoughts into bold execution. The professors of various faiths had room in the broad expanse of his incomparable sway. This was quite different from the practice in other realms, e.g. Persia, Turkey and even Turan.

Akbar's mind was restless as his body; and he delighted in seeking to know the Divine will. He was often absorbed in the intoxicating delight of action. Binyan has narrated that Akbar in his early years "began a habit of disguising himself from time to time and mixing with his subjects in order to hear their opinion of things." After Bairam Khan's ouster and, death, Akbar, although twenty, meant to rule; so he indulged in nocturnal adventures, to satisfy his boundless curiosity.

When opportunity arose in 1561, he gave Maham Anaga a shock by forestalling Adham Khan's actions. He confronted Adham Khan, even when he had come to murder him. Akbar felled him with his fist. Then he ordered his men to throw him from the terrace. When he did not die in the first attempt, he was flung headlong a second time, his neck broken, and his brain scattered. As soon as Maham Anaga learnt of the realities, she shut herself up and wept; her illness grew and she died within six months. Akbar was free to govern. In Abul Fazl's words Akbar "emerged from behind the veil."

Thereafter followed his conciliatory measures, viz. stoppage of enslaving Indian prisoners of war; marriage with Hindu princess; abolition of Pilgrim Tax and stoppage of the practice of levying Zaziya on non-Muslims.

Meeting with Saint Newaldas : The earliest anecdote relating to Akbar's conciliatory moves and his conciliatory spirit has come from Radha Ballabh sect and not from the Jesuit fathers, who concentrated at Agra. The founder of the sect was Srihit Harivansa, who flourshed from 1502 A.D. to 1602 A.D. — a momentous period covering Hemu and Akbar both.[5]

During the pre-Mughal days the Bhakti-cult (devotional cult) rose to its greatest heights. Inspite of loss of vitality and degeneracy due to foreign rule, the influence of this remarkable Bhakti movement enable the Hindu mind to soar to the highest pitch, and give expression to the noblest truths in Literature.

This era of Bhakti movement gave birth to great teachers like Swami Ramanand, Chaitanya Mahaprabhu, Kabir and Nanak. They gave message to the strife torn Hindu society a message of good will and hope. As pointed out by well known historian, Dr. Ishwari Prasad, the philosophical and literacy work of Vaishnavite reformer and other secular writers who flourished in Mithila (Behar), Bengal, and the Deccan, constitute a legacy which the Hindus will always treasure with pride and gratitude.[6]

Ramanandis : The greatest disciple of Swami Ramanand was Kabir and he founded his own *Panth* (sect) known after his name. He was opposed to orthodoxy, both of Hindus as well as Muslims, and with amazing boldness he started his iconoclalstic campaign against religious conventions and idolatory. He laid great emphasis on realisation of God and ideals of pure and simple life. In his epigrammatic and aphoristic style he compared *Sakhis* and *Raginis*, which evince a high order of poetry. In the sphere of religion, Kabir emphasised that though Islam and Hinduism differed in fundamental aspects; but when one looked to God and god alone, the essential underlying unity and oneness comes to the fore.

Some controversy has arisen regarding the exact age in which Kabir lived. According to Dr. P.D. Barthwal, Kabir did not flourish in Sikandar Lodi's reign, i.e. 1489 to 1517 A.D. But on the otherhand Babu Shyam Sundar Das has asserted otherwise in his introduction to *Kabir granthawali*. According to him Kabir composed certain versus which relate to Sikandar Lodi, viz.-

The deity of the Ganges — was deep;
Kabir stood there bound hand and feet,

The ripple broke asunder the fetters and
Kabir was found seated on the deer skin.

According to another anecdote, Sultan Sikander Lodi charged Kabir with blasphemy, when in his presence the saint poet, declared himself to be an incarnation of God. The Qazi tried him and pronounced him to be a *kafir* (infidel). He was however sentenced to death and thrown into the Ganges. The Saint poet escaped drowning by miracle, and was seen seated on a deer-skin above the water of the river.

The Guru Grantha Saheb of the Sikhs also relates the same episode and ascribes the following verses to Kabir, which prove that he was contemporary of Sultan Sikandar Lodi:

Qh! my Lord (Govindra!) Your might is my support.
The Qazi ordered the elephant to be set upon me.
My arms were tied firmly, ... but ...
The elephant was in rage and struck me on the head,
after a while it ran away screaming, for this I am grateful to the Lord.
Oh! the driver ! I Shall strike you with a cudgel, and at the same time the ego in me.
I saw that the elephant did not hurt me,
On the otherhand, it began to pray,
because of divinity in him.
I see the elephant fixed in meditation on me but the blind *qazi* does not understand the miracle wrought by the heavenly power.[7]

Sultan Sikander Lodi excelled without any doubt as an iconoclast and a champion of the faith — orthodoxy bordering on iconoclasm. He became a promoter of an expansionist policy at the cost of the Hindu kingdoms in Madhya Pradesh, Baghelkhand, Oudh and neighbouring States. He conducted the campaigns with ruthless ferocity. His favourites were the theologions and Mullas. He was God-fearing and benevolent to only the Muslim subjects. He aspired to be a paragon of justice. He said in congregation. He built mosques in most of his *Subahs* (Provinces) and territories. He also appointed koran reader, *Khatibes*, and sweepers and consigned stipends to them. He distributed clothing and shawls every winter to *faqirs*. As a result of his iconoclastic policy, nobles and Shaikhs from Arabia, Persia and various parts emigrated to India. Imbibed with iconoclastic zeal, the Sultan raged to the ground, good many temples of the Hindus specially in Mathura, and tried to stifle the Bhakti Movement.

Sikandar's zeal for Islamic expansionism surpassed all bounds. He got temples demolished and even, banned public bathing at Mathura ghats. he built an inn, a *madrasa* and mosques in the predominantly Hindu locality in Mathura and thus deprived the Hindus of bathing grounds. He even banned barbers from shaving the heads of Hindus on auspicious or other important occasions. But such measures could not be effective.

Radhaballabhis : As mentioned earlier, noted Saint, Sri Hit Haribans founded the Radhabalabhis sect. The Krishna cult had been initiated by the famous South Indian devotee, Ballabhacharya. The Radhaballabhi Sect had its precursors in Vidyapati Thakur in Mithila (Bihar) and Vithaldas in Mathura — Brindaban (the famous Brijbhumi). The tradition of euloging Radhaballabh was carried on in the Deccan by Namadeva, whose contemporary was Dnyanoba, who wrote a paraphrase of Srimad Bhagvad Gita.

Ramanand had already preached Rama Cult, and Ballabhacharya became the greatest exponent of Vaishnavism, i.e. Krishna Cult. Born in the South in 1479 A.D. he visited Mathura and Brindaban as well as other holy places in northern India. He finally settled in Varanasi. The celebrated Bengali reformer Chaitanya Mahaprabhu, born in 1485 A.D. was contemporary of Ballabhacharya. He also denounced casteism and preached the universal brotherhood of man. His highest deity was Krishna Radhaballabh whose eternal abode was Gokul.

In the devotional teachings of Namadeva, Kabir and Guru Nanak, there was no place for casteism, polytheism and idolatory. They all condemned casteism and pleaded for faith, sincerety and piety of life. But with the propagation of Krishan Cult by Ballabh, stage was set for the rise of Radhaballabhis, which could attract attention of Hindus as well as Muslims. Rai Puran Mal and Newal Kishore Bhargavas from Rewari came and settled down at

Mathura to preach Radhaballabhi sect. No doubt they came to be known as Purandas and Newal Das. Purandas was beheaded in 1557 A.D., as he was father of Hemu, the arch enemy of the Mughals. However after the exit of Bairam Khan, in 1561, Akbar imbued by conciliatory spirit, came under the influence of Newal Das who was near relation of Hemu and hailed from Rewari.

Bhakti Cult in Rajasthan : Although Purandas and Newal Das were initiated into Radhaballabhi Sect, subsequent to 1533 A.D. i.c. seven yeas after the first battle of Panipat, they were influenced by Bhakti Movement, which was already in full swing in Rajasthan. James Tod has mentioned that Ballabhacharya extensively toured Rajasthan States, and collected a many as seven images of Krishna from various places. He has listed the names and subsequent abodes of the seven statutes of Krishna-Kanaihya, which are as follows:[8]

(i) Nathji : at *Nathdwara* the God Govardhan Nath the God of the famous mount near Mathura NONITA = In this Krishna has been shown as a child with *Peda* (Sweetmeat) in his hand. The original statue had been thrown into the river Jamuna by Muslim invaders. Nathdwara is a famous place of pilgrimage in northern India.

(ii) Mathuranath : *Kota*, where it had been established after having been found at Khamnote in Mewar.

(iii) Dwar-ca-Nath : *Kankerowal*: It was obtained from the house of a Brahimin family of *Kannauj in U.P.* Its whereabout was revealed to Ballabhacharya in dream. It was said to have been adored in Satya-Yuga by a Solar prince.

(iv) Gokul-Nath, or Gokul — Chandrama — at *Jaipur*. This statue was found deep in a ravine in the Jamuna near Gokul. Ballabhacharya obtained the same and got that installed at Jaipur. It was assigned by Ballabh to his own brother in-law.

(v) Yadu Nath: this is the family deity of the kings of Yada vansh. Prior to the invasion of Muslims it was installed somewhere in Mahaban near Mathura. Mahmud Ghaznavi is reported to have demolished that and thrown away. Ballabhacharya got it re-installed in *Surat*.

(vi) Vithal — Nath : Vithalnath alias *Pandurang of Maharashtra*. Ballabhachrya after obtaining the same from the bed of Ganges at Varanasi in 1516 A.D., got that installed (1572 V.E.).

(vii) Mudhun — Mohuna: The beloved of, Radha and the Gopies. A female priest used to get its puja performed earlier. It has been got re-installed in *Jaipur*.

All the above-mentioned shrines and their restoration at the instance of Ballabhacharya and his disciples go to show the revivalist trends in medieval Hindu Society. Rajasthan thus became a nucleus for regeneration and restoration of Hindu ethos. Having got shrines re-established in safer places in Rajasthan, the saints turned their attention to Brij. the original abode of Lord Krishna.

Hemu's Father initiated : It was during this era of reconciliations and unprecedented revival of spiritualism, accompanied by devotional cult (Bhakti movement) amongst the Hindus that Hemu's father Rai Puran Mal was born. When Hemu grew up and Mewat was torn asunder by Afghan-Mughal conflict, Puran Mal resigned and took to asceticism. *He became a fervent disciple of Sri Hit Haribansa at Mathura.* According to Bhagwat Mudit, Dewan of Subedar Shuja-ul-mulk, of Agra, Rai Puran Mal renamed as Puran Das was deputed to Thatta in Sindh to preach teachings of Radhaballabhi sect to Raja Parmanand, who was a mansabdar there.

In Parmananddas *Parichai* (Introduction) Bhagwat Mudit, the author of *Ananya Rasikmal,* has written that Purandas, was an ascetic and was imbued with Sri Hitharibans teachings. By God's inspiration, or by the command of Hit-haribans, Purandas went to Thatta in Sindh, where people were happy to have his *darshan.* The Raja was happy to hear about his qualities; and Purandas was accorded all respect.[9]

Fuller details about Raja Parmanand are lacking. However it is known that he was Kshatriya by caste and an employee of Humayun padshah. He was accorded the status of Mansab-Jagirdar, entitled to keep five hundred infantry. Due to his good work he was promoted to the status of Teen Hazari.

It is not evident from records of Humayun's time as to when he was deputed to Thatta.(Sindh). How ever when Humayun was involved in a struggle against Bahadur Shah of Gujarat, he had contacts in Sindh, Multan, Gakkhar and Amarkot. It is quite probable that during 1534 and 1543 A.D. Humayun had his sway in Sindh. When he was defeated by Sher Shah in 1540, Mirza Kamran went straight to Kabul, but Humayun took the riverine route from Sindh to Gakhar. It was in 1540 A.D. that Humayun through the assistance of the Mirzas, proceeded to Sindh. The Mughal grandees with him, established contacts with Hakim Shah Argun at Thatta. In 1541 Humayun married Hamida Bano Begum and proceeded again towards Thatta. it was during this uncertain period of fugitiveness, that on 15th October 1543, Hamida gave birth to Akbar at Amarkot.

But due to the murder of Shah Husain Argun, by his own soldiers, Humayun decided to proceed towards Kandhar. So between 1534 and 1543 A.D. it is probable that Raja Parmanand was stationed at Thatta on behalf of Humayun padshah. Accordingly Purandas might have joined Raja Parmanand at Thatta in 1535 A.D. According to the poet, Bhagwat Mudit, Raja Parmanand kept him for long.

Raja Parmanand felt greatest delight due to the presence of Purandas, specially when he read out "*Sadachar Bhagwat*" to him. After twelve years stay Purandas expressed his desire to return to Mathura Brindaban. According to *Parmanand parichai*, Purandas must have lived at Thatta from 1535 to 1545 A.D. After the exit of Humayun and installation of Islam Shah Sur, Purandas thought it expedient to return to Mathura Brindaban. This was exactly the time when Hemu rose to eminence under Islam Shah Sur.

Between 1543 and 1547 A.D. Purandas must have returned from Thatta. Raja Parmanand also followed suit. Thanks to blessings of Sri Haribans, both of them revelled in having glimpses of Radha Ballabh Lal. The poet admits that he is unable to explain the celestial glory of the ecstacy of the devotees. Purandas succeeded in imbuing Parmanand with the piety of the songs of Hit Haribans.[10]

Reacting to references in "*Radha Ballabh Sampradaya — Sidhanta and Sahitya.*" by Vijayendra Snatak, Ved Prakash Garg from Muzaffarnagar, in one of his articles has expressed some doubt, as there is no anecdote or couplets separately for Purandas. But as Hemu's father had been executed by Maulana Pir Muhammad it was not an easy affair for Bhagwat Mudit, Dewan of Subedar Shuja-ul-Mulk to eulogise him separately. However Abul Fazl has immortalised his saintliness and devotion to his religion, for which he preferred to die.

Akbar — Newaldas' anecdote: Bhagwat Mudit has narrated Newaldas' encounter with Akbar in full. According to the couplets Newaldas was the disciple of Sir Hit Haribans. He belonged to Dhusar — Bhargava family of Rewari. His father's name was Jagannath and in the geneological table of his family he has been put down as Newal Kishore. After his induction into Bhakti cult he was known as Newaldas. He spent most of his time in *Katha-Kirtan*. He was extremely polite and devoted to the service of saints.[11]

When Newaldas reached Brindaban, he met Sri Hit Haribans and did yeomen service to him. He became his teacher and after testing him several times, gave him *guru-mantra*. He was taught the tenets of other sects also. He was totally renunciated and imbued with the nectar of Sri Radhaballabh's celestial love. He used to enchant the hearts of other devotees. He saw God, within and without. To him profit and loss had equal meaning. Alround the fame of Newaldas spread and no one was so large-hearted as he was. He was endeared to Sri Hit Haribans, as well as to other devotees. After lavishing the above praise Bhagwat Mudit narrates one miracle that he performed.

According to the poet the miracle was shown when Humayun Padshah has breathed his last due to accidental fall from the staircase of the citadel.

Subsequently Hemu (Hem Chandra Vikramaditya) ruled a few days; followed by the rule of Akbar. Having executed Hemu, Akbar assumed the exalted title of Ghazi.

As an aftermath to Hemu's defeat in the second battle of Panipat and his execution, Akbar's lieutenants ordered that his followers be got arrested. The soldiers arrested first the Dhusar Baniyas (Dusre of Vaish community) from Rewari and adjoining territories. When the Mughals learnt that they were other than Hemu's family members and his community men, they ordered their release and arrest of the genuine ones. The soldiers then arrested Hemu's family members and his community people. They were about two hundred from Rewari alone. They were under hiding and were made prisoners. As hundreds had fled, they were subjected to torture and questioning; so that they might diulge the whereabouts of others.

H.A. Phadke in his latest work on *Haryana : Ancient and Medieval*, (1990) has mentioned that "The prisons of Delhi and Agra were filled up with hundreds of Hemu's supporters and followers to be released only when Akbar decided to follow a liberal policy in religious matters." But he has not consulted *Hemu and His Times*, in which it had been clearly mentioned that the Mughals ordered the arrest of all Kinsmen of Hemu, popularly known as Dhusar Bhargava.[12]

As many as two hundred families were affected, the rest of the community members, who were activtists and probably had participated in the battles of Delhi and Panipat, fled east-wards.

As a result of the general massacre in the decisive battle of Panipat, and terror struck by Maulana Pir Muhammad and Bairam Khan, Bhargava Dhusars went underground and remained in hiding for years to come. However after arrests in Rewari and other places, it was reported to the boy emperor that not an individual Dhusar was left in and around Rewari, only one Dhusar ascetic was remaining at Brindaban. The boy emperor ordered him to be brought before him. When he confronted Akbar, he was asked to state his caste and occupation. To this the ascetic saint replied that he knew no caste, he was a devotee of Hari-Krishna and prayer was his only pre-occupation.[13]

Imprisonment and escape:

The reply given by Newaldas to the emperor was regarded as insolent, and he was ordered to be thrown into the prison. While in confinement, Newaldas is reported to have indulged in prayers — recited *Kirtan* (devotional songs) and despite the rigours of the prison, he continued to sing the praises of Hari-Krishna and Shyam. According to the poet Bhagwat Mudit, one day, date and year not specified, a miracle happened, and the saint disappeared from the prison cell. He was reported to have reached Brindaban physically and was busy in the midst of other devotees. When Akbar learnt of that he felt repentent and expressed his desire to summon him to his presence. This time the emperor was inclined to honour him and not prosecute him. He wanted to see the saint in person.

Although the poet has described the meeting that took place at considerable length, but he has not specified when this took place. From the records available it is likely that such a meeting took place when Akbar was on a hunting trip to Mathura and Brindaban, and decided to abolish Pilgrim taxes etc. Jehangir in his Memoirs has also recorded that his father Akbar, "was always associated with the learned of every creed and religion, especially with Pandits and the learned of India, and although he was illiterate, so much became clear to him through constant intercourse with the learned and wise, in his conversations with them, that no one knew him to be illiterate, and he was so acquainted with the niceties of verse and prose compositions that his deficiency was not thought of."[14]

Issue of A Firman : According to the anecdote of Newaldas Akbar was so impressed with the talk that he requested Newaldas to ask for something; which was to be awarded by means of a *firman*. Accordingly the saint Newaldas advised the emperor to release all those kinsmen and community people belonging to Hemu's caste, as that did not fulfil any purpose. Akbar thereupon not only ordered general amnesty to all, but also bestowed upon the only surviving member of Hemu's family, the Qanungoi of the pargana Kanaud in the sircar of Narnaul.

As the Firman of Akbar dated 8 Mahi-i-Mihr Ilahi, dated 1563 A.D., has been traced, the authenticity of the poet's anecdote relating to Akbar's munificence at the instance of Newaldas should be accepted. The National Archives of India exhibited photo copy of the *firman* in EKTA exhibition of select documents and photographs on the basic unity of India, in the Archives Week, Nov. 29 to Dec. 5, 1984.

In addition to the above *firman* geneological tables of Hemu's descendents, Trilockchand, Rai Narain Das and Nathmal have been published. That establishes the real origin of Hemu and nullifies the calumy showered on him by the Mughal chroniclers.

It is high time that with the unearthing of documentary evidences, the *firman*, the geneological tables and the Hindi manuscripts of the poet Bhagwat Mudit all fanciful stories of the low origin of Hemu should be set at rest.

Much has been written on religious views of Akbar, his *Sulahkul, Din-i-Ilahi*, but very little has been brought to light about his earliest experiences with Saints and *faqirs* in and around Agra. The deciphering of the date of *firman* is significant as that establishes Akbar's munificence and catholicity after having been freed from the tutelage of Bairam Khan, subsequent to his murder at Patan by an Afghan.

A sketch depicting Akbar, of early age i.e. about twenty years, at the time of his receiving blessings of Newaldas has come to light from the descendents of Hemu. The same is published. The sketch seems to be correct, so far as his age at 1563 A.D. does not appear to be more than twenty.

Akbar's benevolent policy : The young Mughal emperor's catholicity and respect for the Hindu saints, coupled with his matrimonial alliance with Rajput ladies led to peaceful devotional activities in and around Delhi, Agra and Mathura. This is amply corroborated by construction of several temples erected and dedicated to Radha.[15] The founder is also credited with compilation of a manual entitled Radha Sudha Nidhi, which is a series of Sanskrit verses in praise of Radha. A collection of songs and an exposition of the notions of the sect is found in Seve Sakhi Vana in Hindi having forty sections.

Besides the above there are several other works in Braj Bhasha, which have been continuously regulating or inspiring the devotion of the worshippers of Radha Vallabha. As mentioned earlier a descriptive account of such devotees is contained in *Ananya Rasik Mal* and *Hit Charita* composed by Bhagwat Mudit.

As a result of the reconciliation of Dhusar Bhargavas, several of them received or obtained landed property in the parganas in Mathura, Bulandshahr, Gurgaon and several other Sarkars. A number of them rose to high posts under the Mughal emperor. Out of these Rao Sujan Singh Bhargava was quite prominent. He was a resident of Qutubpur — Rewari and remained a high dignitary in the eighteenth century in Mathura and Koel (Aligarh). His descendents still reside at Aligarh. His family became well known as "Chahladan". Rao Sujan Singh was very brave. Subsequently he came under the influence of Saint Charandas and became his disciple.

At the time of Akbar's death in 1605 A.D., Baval area adjacent to Delhi, was under Raja Dhumimal Bhargava. His son Raja Chittarmal and his descendents continued to enjoy the estate till 1715 when Raja Jatwal was the beneficiary. It was only after 1845 A.D. that his descendents migrated to Uttar Pradesh and settled in places like Aligarh, Saharanpur etc.,

The ancestors of the famous saint of Delhi Charandas also hailed from Dehra in Alwar, and Shobhandas was a contemporary of Hemu's father Rai Purandas. Charandas carried on the devotional traditions of his family and rose to eminence when Nadirshah invaded Delhi. He was very well respected and honoured by the then Mughal emperor, Muhammad Shah.

The benefits accruing under the *firman* granted by Akbar continued to be enjoyed by Kanaudia Bhargava till the eighteen-fifty seven revolt, when due to their having sided with Nawab of Jhajhar and bestowal of the area to the Sikh ruler of Patiala, they lapsed. Thanks to the reconciliation attempted by Akbar, Mahipal's descendents enjoyed the benefits for full 367 years. However some lands in Kanaud now known as Mahendragarh are still in possession of Dhusar Bhargavas. All attempts by Dharma Mitra Bhargava to seek restoration of grants in the line of Qannugo and Nankar rights in Kanaud from Raja of Patiala in Jaunary 1924 A.D. failed.

Notes and References

1. *Rise and fall of the Mughal Empire*. p. 229. Bihari Mal had met Akbar, while he was camping near Kalali, on way to the shrine of Muinuddin Chishti on 24th January 1562 and offered the hand of his daughter in marriage.
2. *Ain-i-Akbari*, p. 203
3. Binyan, Lawrence; *Akbar*., p. 16 also *Jahangir-nama*, p. 37 trs. Alexander Rogers, edited by Henry Beveridge, 1968.
4. Ibid; p. 63.
5. Tripathi, R.N. *Kavita Kaumudi* Vol. I pp. 221 (1923 ed.) also see, Vijayendra Snatak, *Radhaballabhi Sampradaya — Sidhanta and Sahitya*; 2014 V.E. (1957 A.D.) According to this Sri Hit Haribans was born in 1559 V.E. (1502 A.D.).
6. *Medieval India*., pp. 513-514.
7. Roy, Nirodbhushan., *Neamatullah's History of the Afghans* (trs.) 1958: Santiniketan, West Bengal, Addendum, pp.210-211.
8. *Annals and Antiquities of Rajasthan*, or the Central and Western Rajput states of India, Vol.I. 1957 (ed.) pp. 426-438.
9. *Ananya Rasikmal*: ed. Lalitaprased purohit, pp. 22-24. Anecdote relating to Sri Parmananddas and Saint Purandas.
10. Ibid. p. 24.
11. Ibid. p. 15.
12. *Hemu and His Times*, 1961 pp. 137-138.
13. *Bhagwat Mudit*., *Rasik Ananyamal*, (ed.) Lalita Prasad Purohit, pp. 15-18, Newaldas Anecdote. See, Appendix C for Hindi version reproduced.
14. *Jahangir-Nama*, (Trs.) Rogers & Beveridge, p.33
15. Growse, *Mathura : A District Memoir*, Pt.I. pp. 120-121. According to it the Radha ballabhis have a temple at Brindaban dedicated to Krishna, said to have been built in the year 1585 A.D., by Hari Vansh, the founder of the sect, a native of Deobund in the district of Saharanpur. There are several inscriptions rudely scrawled on the walls, but the oldest at present invisible bears the date of Sambat, 1684 VE i.e. 1627

A.D. 9Fn. 15 contd) *The Satistical, Descriptive and Historical Accounts* of the North-West Provinces of India: *Mathura*, pt. I. 1884 A.D. pp. 103-104, also mentions that Krishna Chand Girham built a temple at Radhamohan, which is still in possession of his descendents. Whilst Brij Chand was the ancestor of the present Gosains of the temple of Radha Vallabh, the Chief shrine of the sect.

Epilogue

Hemu's rise was meteoric. He flashed and blazed forth like lightening. His fame and glory dazzled the eyes of his contemporaries. He shone for a while like a silver lining amidst the dark clouds but his eclipse was equally sudden and unexpected. Born of a saintly father, belonging to a Dhusar Bhargava family, he rose to be a non-pereil general, a warrior, a victor, a conqueror and an outstanding commander. His tactical moves, his mode of attack and his organizational skill baffled his enemies. Having earned the appellation of Raja Bikramajit, he rose to be the king of Delhi, nay the last Hindu emperor of India.

Being a worthy son of a devotee father, Hemu imbibed all the traits of catholicity and large-heartedness. He was secular to the core. He was respected equally by Hindu and Muslims, revered as well as honoured by Rajputs and Afghans. Inspite of having a puny physique, unassuming personality, he had a commanding voice. He could shout exultantly in the midst of a battle. He succeeded in overpowering his adversaries, however redoubtable they were. Either in the battle-field or in the banquet hall he was always vociferous and kept on exhorting all those present to heights of valour and warriorship.

Hemu was possessed of a dynamic and magnetic personality. The phenomenon of his rise to prime-ministership of Adil Shah Sur and his accession to the throne of Delhi, was unique in Medieval history. He remained in the forefront in Northern India for a period of three to five years. When the country was torn by internecine warfare between the Afghan nobles, anarchy reigned alround, it was he, who rose to the occasion to restore law and order, and maintain the dignity of the throne of Delhi. As a conqueror of twenty-two battles Hemu defeated the Mughal forces at the battle of Delhi also known as battle of Tughluqabad and finally ended his career as a martyr of Panipat. Its a pity that Babur, the victor of the first battle of Panipat, paid due respect to Ibrahim Lodi, the martyr, and allowed erection of his tomb at very place, but his grandson did nothing of the sort.

The detailed accounts by the contemporary chronicler, have immortalised the valour and deeds of Hemu, a Hindu general. His preparations of war, and the meticulous details worked out by him at Tughluqabad and Panipat excite wonder of readers even today. His main achievement lay in harnessing as many as fifteen hundred elephants, out of whom at least five hundred were war-mad. It was indeed a stupendous task to keep together such a big force, feed them, arrange for their armour and above all finance them. No wonder Badaoni has accused Hemu of feeding the mountain like war-elephants, with rice, oil (butter) and sugar when famine and pestilence was raging alround Agra, Bayana and even Delhi. Yet the wars had to be won, order had to be restored and the throne of Delhi kept secure. This could not be possible without all the measures adopted by Hemu in the hour of crisis or national emergency. He was indeed performing miracles when he was keeping a locust-like army, of fifty thousand cavalry, 1500 elephants and thousands of infantry men in battle order. All chroniclers are unanimous in their praise of his preparations and the success achieved by him was due to an unparalled accumulation of arms, ammunitions, and treasures with no end or measure.

Hemu was pains-taking and indefatigable, though did not know much of horse-riding, he is reported to have become accustomed to being fastened to the *howdah* of the elephants. It was indeed a wonder in the sixteenth century for Hemu to move his troops, to and fro from Ajmer in the West to Khawaspur Tanda in the East, from Karnal to Bayana and Alwar to Sambhal. It is difficult to apportion time taken by him in traversing so distant places with hardly any roads or other means of communication, except horses and elephants. In short Hemu's war-animals must have been prodigals or paragon of swiftness, failing which in less than three years he could not have conquered twenty-two battles.

Hemu was farsighted. He knew that order could be restored only if the recalcitrant Afghans nobles could be kept together. What a surprise that where Islam Shah and Adli Shah failed, Hemu succeeded in keeping them united against the Mughals! However he knew no soft-pedling. He knew that the adversaries and warring factions, whether Rajputs or Afghans, could be kept in check by a strong hand. Hence he did not hesitate to put them down, to hunt them down and drive them right upto the confines of the then Bengal. He ousted Ibrahim Sur from his strong hold and kept Sikandar Sur at a distance. Hemu did not take precipitate action, after the sudden death of Humayun, he waited for the opportunity and attacked the Mughals after full preparations. Even at the hour of triumph he did not lose patience, he did not pursue the fleeing Mughal generals after the battle of Delhi. He avoided risky pursuits and always consolidated his positions, before taking further action. His farsightedness was a key to his success.

Hemu was essentially a product of the sixteenth century, and has rightly been hailed as "as the most remarkable man of the century." He lived in the age of great warriors, like Rana Sanga, Babar, Sher Shah and subsequently Rana Pratap; so his fame had been stultified due to grandiloquent accounts of their performances. Hemu's span of activities amongst all the above generals was the shortest, yet his achievements excelled most of them. None of them could claim to be a victor of all the battles he fought. Besides that the Rajputs, the Mughal and the Sur generals had a command of a homogeneous army, but Hemu had a hetrogeneous army. to fight with. Religious affinity also played an important part, but Hemu mobilised a truly secular army consisting of Rajputs, Afghans and his community men, the fewest in number.

The courtier historians and their contemporaries have exhausted all their rhetoric and vulgar vocabulary in pouring their venom on Hemu, calling him bad names. Yet in their overzealousness to exalt their hero, the boy Mughal emperor, they have recorded details, without which Hemu's greatness could not be known to posterity.

Although Abul-Fazl took pains to record his birth place and his father's execution, but he did not mention that he belonged to a respectable middle class land-owner's family. That Hemu's parents lived in Narnaul and so had intimate relations with Farid, the *Sakin-i-Narnaul* and the same was reflected in Islam Shah's respect to Hemu and Adil Shah's total reliance on him. No historian has reflected upon this difference in Sur King's attitude towards Hindu minister, specially when the Afghan nobles were humiliated and harangued at every step by Islam Shah. This factor alone entitles Hemu to be ranked amongst the most respected secular leader in the sixteenth century. Recent investigations have brought to light not only the geneology of Hemu, but also of Ramayya, his sister's son. So Hemu was not alone as a general, he wasassisted by Rai Mahipal and Ramayya. Akbar did the wisest thing in recognising Nathmal the infant heir of Mahipal, Hemu's nephew, as the rightful beneficiary for the bestowal of the Qanungoi of Pargana Kanauda, in the Sarkar of Narnaul. The original *farman* has since been traced. The qanungoi rights were enjoyed by his descendents till the eighteen-fifty seven revolt, when the Britishers abrogated them, and appropriated them to other rulers. Some of the descendents of Hemu even now have landed property in Kanaud, better known as Mahendragarh.

Last but not the least fanciful causes have been ascribed for Hemu's defeat. But the real assessment has been summed up by the distinguished historian, Dr. R.P. Tripathi in two sentences. He says, "The causes of his defeat, were the capture of his artillery and the random arrow, which made him unconscious and caused panic in his army. His defeat was accidental and victory of Akbar providential." Akbar's destiny was respledent and his most formidable rival, and hero of the Afghans, disappeared from the political chess-board with one shot. No wonder the Mughals celebrated the occasion by the execution of almost a dead man, proclamation of Akbar, the emperor, as Ghazi and despatch of his head to be hung at the iron gates of Kabul and his body (trunk) was thrown away in Delhi. However the martyrdom of Hemu could not be washed away despite four hundred years of calumny and vilification. It undoubtedly paved the way for the re-establishment of Mughal dynasty by Bairam Khan and the glorification of Akbar. Inspite of all that happened or might have happened, the hard fact remains that Hemu lived a glorious life, and his brief but eventful military career, crowned by twenty-nine days rule at Delhi will ever remain memorable in the annals of the world.

[illegible] in India. However [illegible] [illegible] [illegible] [illegible] [illegible] [illegible] life, and [illegible] [illegible] of the world.

Bibliography

I. Primary Sources

(a) *Afghan Sources*

(1) Tarikh-i-Sher Shahi, by Abbas Sarwani. Eng. trs. in Elliot and Dowson, IV pp. 305-433.

(2) Tarikh-i-Khan Jahani wa Makhzan-i-Afghania, Engl. trs. by B. Dorn in the History of the Afghans (1829) and by Nirodbhushan Roy, Santineketan 1950.

(3) Tarikh-i-Daudi by Abdulla. Eng. trs. in part in Elliot and Dowson. IV pp. 434-513 based on Waqiat-i-Mushtaqi, i.e. History of the Afghan rulers of India upto the year 1575-76.

(4) Tarikh-i-Salatin-i-Afghania or the Tarikh-i-Shahi, by Ahmad Yadgar.

(b) *Non-Afghan and Mughal Sources*

(1) Tazkirat-ul-Waqiat by Jauhar Aftabchi, Eng. trs. by Major C. Stewart, 1832 & 1940.

(2) Tarikh-i-Humayun Shahi by Saikh Ilhadad Faizi Sirhindi.

(3) Humayun-nama by Gulbadan Begum.

(4) Mirat-ul-Mamlik, by Sidi 'Ali Rais. Eng. trs. by A. Vambrey, entitled, The Travels and Adventures of the Turkish Admiral Sidi 'Ali Rais. in India, Afghanistan, Central Asia and Persia during the years, 1553-1556, London 1899.

(5) Akbar Nama, by Shaikh Abul-Fazl, 1596. Eng. trs. H. Beveridge, 1912.

(6) Ain-i-Akbari, by Abul Fazl, compiled before 1602 A.D. Ed. by Blochman, 2 Volumes. Eng. trs. Vol. I. by H. Blochman and Vol. II. and III by H.S. Jarrett.

(7) Muntakhabu-T-Tawarikh by Abul-Qadir Badaoni, Eng. trs. by Ranking, W.H. Lowe and T.W. Haig.

(8) Tabaqat-i-Akbari by Khwaja Nizam-uddin Ahmad, Eng. trs. by B. De entitled, A History of India from the early Musalman invasions to the 38th years of the reign of Akbar.

(9) Tarikh-i-Akbari by Muhammad Arif Qandhari.

(10) Moasir-Rahimi, by Muhammad Abdul Baqi.

(11) Tarikh-i-Feristha, by Ferishta. Eng. trs. by John Briggs, 4 Volumes, entitled Rise of the Mahomedan Power in India till the year 1612 A.D.

(12) Tuzuk-i-Babari, Babur Nama, Eng. trs. John Leyden and William Erskine; also A.S. Beveridge.

(13) Tarikh-i-Mubarak Shahi by Yahiya Bin Ahmad-Bin A. Bin "Å" Sirhindi.

(14) Tuzuk-i-Jahangeri, Eng. trs. by Roger ed. by H. Beveridge, London 1909, Reprinted.

(15) Inayat Nama by Inayat Khan Rasika-Collection of letters and other historical documents.

(16) Daulat-i-Sher Shahi by Hasan Ali Khan.

(17) Khulasat-ul-Tawarikh by Sujan Rai Khattri Ms. Khuda Baksh Library, Patna, written in 1695 A.D.

(18) Lubbat-Tawarikh by Vrindavan Das in 1689, A.S.B. Ms. in Calcutta.

(19) Tabakat-i-Nasiri, 2 Vols. Eng. trs. by Major H.G.P. Raverty, London, 1881 A.D.

(20) Waqiat-i-Mustaqi, by Rizqullah. (21) Tarikh-i-Rashidi, by Muhammad Haidar Dughlat, Eng. trs. Elias and E. Devison, Rose, 1895 A.D.

(22) Maasir-ul-Umra, by Shah Nawaz Khan, A Dictionary of Mughal peerage, careers of nobles and officers of the Mughal period, 1788 A.D.

(23) The Dabistan-i-Mazahib by Musin Fani written in 1648 A.D. is a comparative study of religions that flourished during the Mughal period.

(24) The Bijak of Kabir, by Ahmad Shah, Hamirpur 1917.

(c) *European Sources*

(1) Father A. Monserrates' *Account of Akbar*, (26th November 1582 A.D.) Edited and trs. into English by Fr. H. Hosten in Journal and Proceedings of the Asiatic Society of Bengal, 1912.

(2) De Imperio Magno Mongoli, Sive India Vera, by De Laet, Commentaries ex Variis Auctoribus Congestus Leyden, 1631, trs. into English from Latin version by J.S. Holland and annotated by S.N. Banerji under the title — *The Empire of the Great Mogul.*

(3) Francis Bernier, Travels in the Mogul Empire., 1668.

(4) Nicolao Manucci, Mughal India (1653-1708) or Storio Do Mogar, Four Volumes (Reprint).

(d) *Hindi Sources*

(1) *Dalpat Vilas*, written for Dalpat Singh a contemporary Rajput Chief of Bikaner; covers Akbar's relations with Rajputs.

(2) *Muhanote Naiṅsi, Khyat*, Histọry of Jodhpur in particular and Rajasthan in general ed. by G.H. Ojha, 2 Volumes 1982 V.E.

(3) *Ananya Rasikmal* by Bhagwat Mudit penned by Dungarsi in 1817 V.E. i.e. 1760 A.D., another Mss. was penned down in 1838 V.E. i.e... 1780 A.D. Two such Mss. are available in Manuscript Section of Nagari Pracharni Sabha, Varanasi. There is another published version, from Vrindaban, edited by Lalita Prasad Purohit. Bhagwat Mudit in all probability wrote between 1707 and 1720 V.E. i.e. 1650 and 1663 A.D.

(4) Hit Charita and Ananya Rasikmala, by Bhagwat Mudit.

II. **Secondary Sources**

(1) Azad, M.H., Darbar-i-Akbari (In Urdu, Lahore, 1898) (In Hindi, Varanasi, 1967 A.D.) by Ram Chandra Varma.

(2) Binyan, Lawrence, Akbar.

(3) Banerjee, Humayun Padshah.
(4) Barnett, Lionel David, Hinduism, London 1913.
(5) Bhandarker, R.G., Vaishnavism, Saivism and Minor religious systems, Strassburg, 1913.
(6) Campos, History of the Portuguese Power in India.
(7) Danvers, Fredrick Charles, The Portuguese in India, 2 Volumes, London 1894. Revised Edition also.
(8) Das, Shyam Sunder, Kabir Granthavali, Nagari Pracharnni Sabha, Varanasi.
(9) Dharmamitra, Hemu Veer (In Urdu)
(10) Elphinstone, History of India.
(11) Elliot, Sir Henry M., The History of India as told by its historians, the Mahomedan period ed. John Dawson, 8 Volumes London, 1367.
(12) ----, Historians of Muhammadan India, Vol. I. London 1849.
(13) Erskine, William., A History of India under the first two sovereigns of the House of Timur, Babar and Humayun, 2 Volumes, London, 1854.
(14) Fredrick Augustus, Count of Noer, The Emperor Akbar, Eng. trs. by A.S. Beveridge, Vol. I. Calcutta, 1890.
(15) Garbe, Dr. Richard Von., Akbar, Emperor of India, Chicago, 1909 A.D.
(16) Growse, F.S., Mathura, A District Memoir, 1880.
(17) Habib, Irfan., Agrarian system of Mughal India, Bombay, 1963.
(18) ----, Atlas, Medieval India.
(19) Irvine, W., Army of the Mughals, London, 1903.
(20) Ibbetson, D., Punjab Castes, Lahore, 1916 (Reprint).
(21) Keay, F.E., A History of Hindi Literature, 1920.
(22) Krishnamurti, R., Akbar, the Religious Aspect, Baroda, 1961.
(23) Lane-Poole, Stanley., Medieval India under Muhamaden Rule, London 1810, (Reprint).
(24) ----, Rulers of India, Babur (Reprint).

(25) Maclagan, R., The Jesuits and the Great Mughal, London, 1932.
(26) Malleson, G.B., Akbar, London 1890.
(27) Moreland, W.H., The Agrarian System of Moslem India, Cambridge, 1929 (Reprint).
(28) ----, India at the death of Akbar - An Economic Study, London, 1920 (Reprint).
(29) Olaf Caroe, The Pathans, 550 B.C. to 1957 A.D. (1958) (1963).
(30) Phadke, H.A., Haryana, Ancient and Medieval, 1990.
(31) Prasad, Dr. Beni., Jahangir.
(32) Prasad, Dr. Ishwari, Life and Times of Humayun.
(33) ----, Medieval India.
(34) Qanungo, K.R., Sher Shah.
(35) ----, Sher Shah and His Times, 2nd ed. 1965.
(36) Roy, Nirodbhushan., Neamutullah, History of the Afghans, Part I. Santineketan, 1958.
(37) ----, Sher Shah and his Successors, 1934.
(38) Sarda, Har Bilas, Ajmer, Historical and Descriptive Ajmer, 1911.
(39) ----, Maharana Kumbha, Ajmer, 1917.
(40) ----, Rana Sanga.
(41) Sarkar, Jadunath, Studies in Mughal India, Calcutta, 1919.
(42) Smith, Vincent, Akbar the Great Mogul.
(43) Siddiqi, Iqtidar H., History of Sher Shah, Aligarh, 1971.
(44) Snatak, Vijeyendra, Radha Ballabh Sampradaya, and Sidhanta, 1959. (Hindi).
(45) Sharma, Sri Ram, Religious Policy of the Mughal Emperors, Calcutta, 1940/1962.
(46) ----, Mughal Administration.
(47) Srivastava, Dr. Ashirwadi Lal, The Sultanate of Delhi.
(48) ----, Mughal Empire, & Akbar, 1526-1603 A.D.
(49) ----, Sher Shah and His Successors, Agra, 1950.
(50) Tod, James, Annals and Antiquities of Rajasthan, Two Volumes, Revised Ed.

(51) ----, Rajput Kulon Ka Itihas, Part I Vol. I. ed. Dr. Raghubir (In Hindi), 1963. Mangal Prakashan, Jaipur.

(52) Tripathi, Dr. R.P., Some Aspects of Mughal Administration.

(53) ----, Rise and fall of the Mughal Empire.

(54) Thomas, H.H., Chronicles of the Pathan Kings of Delhi, London, 1871.

(55) Wilson, H.H., Hindu Religion, Published by the Society for the resuscitation of Indian Literature, Calcutta, 1899.

IV. **Periodicals & Magazines,**

(1) EKTA Brochure of the National Archives of India, Archives Week Exhibition, Nov. 29 to Dec. 1984 on the Basic Unity of India, displaying Akbar's Firman to Hemu's descendents.

(2) Punjab History Conference, Proceedings, 1978 Twelfth Session., March 17-19 Patiala, G. Khurana's paper on Location of the Second Battle of Panipat, 1556.

(3) Medieval India — A. Miscellany. Vol. I. Centre of Advanced Study, Dept. of History, Aligarh Muslim University — Iqtidar Alam Khan's article on the Mughal Court Politics during Bairam Khan's Regency, pp. 21-38.

(4) ----, Vol. II. Wajh-i-Ma'Ash Grants under the Afghan Kings, 1451-1555.

(5) ----, Vol. III. Documents of the Sur period.

(6) Calendar of Documents, Dr. Irfan Habib, The Indian Economic and Social Review, Vol. IV. No. 3.

(7) Oriental College Magazine, Vol. IX. No. 3.1933 Sher Shah's Firmans.

(8) Journal, Royal Asiatic Society, Calcutta, 1916. An article by Vincent Smith on The Death of Hemu.

(9) ----, 1968, pp. 29-36. An article by Iqtidar Alam Khan on the nobility under Akbar and the development of Religious policy, 1560-80.

(10) Journal, Asiatic Society, Pakistan, An article by Fazlur Rahman on "Akbar's Religion", 1965.

(11) Proceedings of the All Pakistan History Conference, I. 1951. An article by S.M. Jaffar on "Religious Views of Akbar and Aurangzeb" as disclosed by contemporary archives.,

(12) Jadunath Sarkar Commemoration Volume II. 1958. An Article on "The Rajput empresses of Akbar and Jahangir," by H. Goetz.

(13) Dacca University Studies, Vol. I. 1935. An article on the Death of Hemu, by S. Roy.

(14) Indian Historical Quarterly, 28, 1952. An article on the Execution of Tardi Beg Khan by S. Roy.

(15) Proceedings of the Punjab Indian Historical Conference, 1952, an article by S. Roy on Akbar and The Coup de' etat of March 1560.

(16) Journal of Bihar and Orissa Research Society, 1934. An article by Parmatma Saran on The Date and Place of Sher Shah's Birth.

(17) Journal of Indian History, 40. (1962) An article by Dr. A.L. Srivastava, on Akbar and National Integration.

(18) ----, 42 (1964). An article by Dr. A.L. Srivastava on Some Misconceptions about Akbar the Great.

(19) ----, 46 (April 1968). An article by Dr. A.L. Srivastava on Akbar's Alliance with Akbar - an estimate of Raja Bharmal.

(20) ------, (1921-1922). An article by Dr. P.P. Tripathi on Mahan Anagah and Akbar.

(21) Journal of Indian History, 37 (April 1959). An article on Revenue System of Sher Shah by Satish Chandra Misra.

(22) Islamic Culture, 31 (Oct. 1957), An article on Administrative System of the Surs (Sher Shah and His Successors) by S.C. Misra.

(23) Islamic Review, 1936, An article on The Date of Sher Shah's accession, by N.K. Bhattarali.

(24) Journal of the Asiatic Society of Pakistan, 5, 1960, An article on Date and Place of Sher Shah's accession by Abdul Karim.

V. **Gazetteers :**

Districts of Alwar, Karnal, Agra, Mathura, Farukhabad, Allahabad, Mirzapur, Varanasi, Ajmer.

VI. **Souvenires** of the Local Bhargava Sabhas published at the time of or during the Centenary year of the All India Bhargava Sabha in 1989-90.

Rewari, Jaipur, Delhi, Agra, Kanpur, and Allahabad — containing.

Local history of the Bhargava families, and their geneological tables, including those of Hemu and Ramayya.

APPENDIX A

Geneological Table of Hemu's family

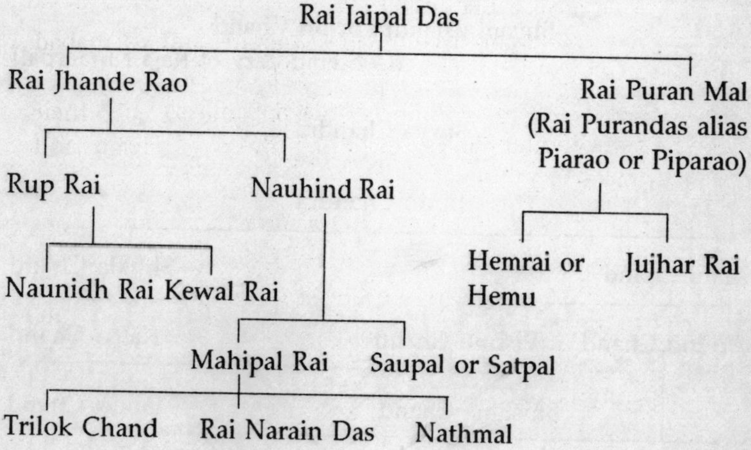

Source : The geneological table has been supplied by the descendents of Rai Narain Das living at present in Jaipur and Rewari. It has also been published earlier by Dharma Mittra, author of *Hemu Veer* in Urdu. Details have also been checked from the Bahis of Pandit Raja Ram of Allahabad, Tirtha Purohita of Kaunadia — Dhusar Bhargavas.

APPENDIX B (i)*

Geneological table of Ramayya, Hemu's sister's son

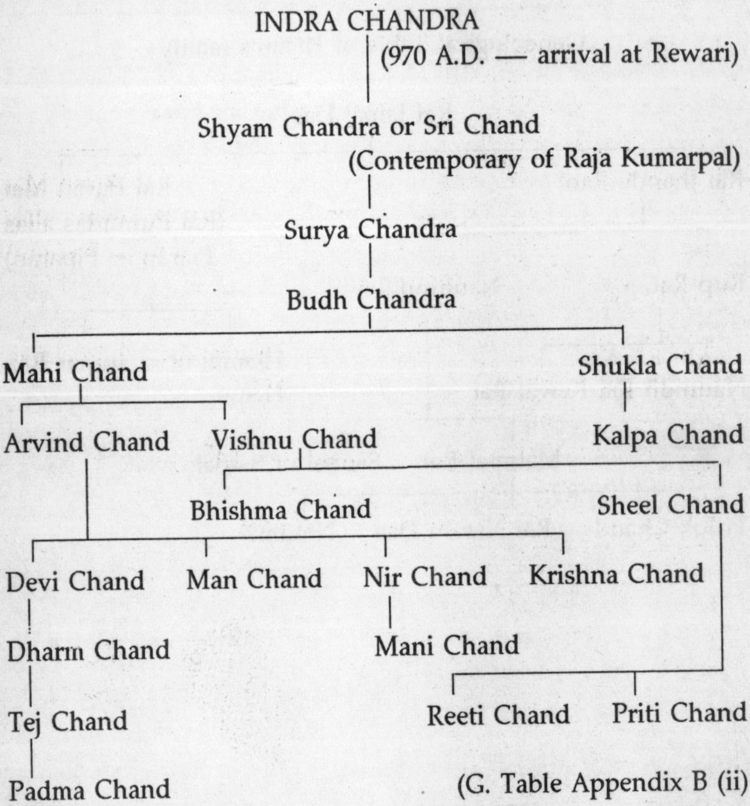

Source : *Smarika* (Sonvenier — Bhargava Local Sabha Rewari-1989. Article by Dr. Manhar Gopal).

Ramyya ---- Hemu's sister's son.

APPENDIX B (ii)

PRITI CHAND

(Contemporary of Prithvi Raj Chauhan)

- Madhur Chand
  - Griva Chand
    - Shiva Chand
      - Man Chand
        - Nam Chand
          - Abhiram Chand
            - Shayam Chand
              - Vikral Chand (By adoption)
                - Jalla Chand
                - Prithvi Chand
                - Sri Chand
                  - Vasu Chand
                    - Vijai Chand
                    - Kama Chand
                    - Jivamal
                  - Lekh Chand
                    - Gokul Chand
                      - Gun Chand
                        - Ram Chand RAMYYA
                          - Mam Chand (Died fighting)
                          - Parva Chand (Died fighting)
                          - Pushya Chand or Pushya Rai (Only surviver)
                        - Shyam Chand (Died fighting)
                        - Krishna Chand (Died fighting)
                        - Vishnu Chand (Died fighting)
                        - Hanu Chand (Died fighting)
                        - Ravi Chand (Died fighting)
                      - Jeevannath
                      - Mahinath
                        - Beni Nath (Died fighting)
                        - Budh Nath (Died fighting)
                        - Prithvi Nath (Died fighting)
        - Dham Chand
        - Kain Chand
        - Bain Chand
  - Gandhra Chand
    - Tulya Chand
- Ras Chand
  - Rudra Chand
    - Shukra Chand

APPENDIX C
NEWALDAS ANECDOTE
नव्ल दास की कथा[1]

दोहा : अब श्री हित हरिवंश के सिष्य नवल हैं जान।
दूसर कुल पावन कियौ, तिनकौ करौ बषान ॥१॥
चौपाई : रैवारी मधि घर है तिनकौ। कथा कीरतन मैं मन तिनकौ ॥२॥
साधन की सेवा सुठि करैं। महानम्र सबकौ मन हरैं ॥३॥
सत संगति वृंदावन आए। श्री हरिवंश मिलैं सुष पाए ॥4॥
बहुत घौस लौ सेवा कीनो। गुरु ने सिष्य परिछ्या लींनी ॥५॥
तब निजु मंत्र सुनायौ जाकौ। धर्म अनन्य बतायो ताकौ ॥६॥
महा विरक्त जुगल रस भीनौं। जथा लाभ संतोष न हीनौ ॥७॥
श्री राधा बल्लभ के गुनगावै । रसिक जननि के चित्त चुरावै ॥८॥
बाहिर भीतर प्रभु कौं देषैं। हानि लाभसुष दुष सम लेषै ॥९॥
जहां तहां फुरै नबल कौ भाव । गुनही गुन नहिं वेकौ चाव ॥१०॥
छुआ त्रषा के वस नहिं सोई । अति अगाध हिय ल है न कोई ॥११॥
गुौ हरि साधनि सुषद सुभाई । काल भजन बिनु बृथा न जाई ॥१२॥
और सुनौ कौतुक इक नीकौ । परेचें भयौ नवलजन जी कौ ॥१३॥
हुमयुं शाह जब गढ़ गिर मरो । हेम राज कछुक दिन करौ ॥१४॥
बहरि अकबर को भयौ राज । हेमू मारयो बैठयो बैठयो गाज ॥१५॥
साह कही वनियनि कौ लावहु । मारौ सवनि जहां लगि पावहु ॥१६॥
अहदी गए पकरि सब लाए । आन झरोषैं तरै दिषाए ॥१७॥
तब उजीर ने बिनती कीनी । चूक सवैं दूसर सिर दीनी ॥१८॥
वनक छोरि तब दूसर पकरे। ढूढि ढूढि वेरिनु मैं जकरे ॥१९॥
हेमु कुल पकरन को धाए । द्वैं सत रैंवारी ते ल्याए ॥२०॥
बंदी किये बहु त्रास दिषाए । दुरे छिपैं ते तिननि बताए ॥२१॥
दूसर तौ अब कोई नाही । एक रह्यो वृन्दावन माही ॥२२॥
तब वृन्दावन अहदी आए । नवलदास कौ ले पहुचाए ॥२३॥
पातसाह ने बूझी बात । कहिरे नवल आपनी जात ॥२४॥
नवल कही जिन पदा किये । अब उन पर अपने करि लिये ॥२५॥
जाति न कोई भए अतीत । हरी भक्तिनि की औरि रीति ॥२६॥
साह कही अब बाधैं तोहि । न्यारी रीति दिषावत मोहि ॥२७॥

1. Bhagwat Mudit, Rasik Ananyamala–Mss, Nagari Pracharni Sabha Collection of Manuseripts : Writer Dungarsi–date of writing. 1817 A.D.

साषी : नवलकृत

जो कोउ जरें जंजीरन तो तोरो सत सात ।
प्रेम तंत अटक्यौ नवल मटक्यो तनक न जात ॥२८॥
चौपाई : साह न समभयौं नवल जु कह्यौ । अर्थ उजीर कहैं ते लह्यौ ॥२९॥
सुनत साह जंजीर मंगाई । पग अरु हार गुदी मैं नाई ॥३०॥
बांधि जंजीर दियौ वंद साला । मारि कपाट लगायौ ताला ॥३१॥
जल अरु अन्नजानि नहि पावें । ह्वांई नवल स्याम गुनगावें ॥३२॥
गुरु पद इष्ट धाम चित लायो । देह सहित वृन्दावन आयी ॥३३॥
तीन दिना पाछे सुधि लीनी । सब जंजीर कोठे मधिचीन्ही ॥३४॥
फिरि के अहदी साहि पटायौ । नवल बहुरि वृन्दावन पायौ ॥३५॥
अहदी कही जु साह बुलाए । परमारथहित नवल जु आए ॥३६॥
करामात तुम प्रगट दिषाई । ताते मो मन दया जु आई ॥३७॥
अग़्या करौ सोई परमान । ढूसर क्यौं रोके बिन जान ॥३८॥
जो कोई करें सोई फल पावे । क्यो इनका तू बृथा सतावे ॥३९॥
ऐसे उपदेस्यों बहुग्यान । दूसर सब छुटवाए आन ॥४०॥
अपने अपने घरनि पठाए । तबते दूसर भक्त कहाए ॥४१॥
साह नवल कौ आदर कीनौं । डिग बै ठाइ प्रेम रस भीनौं ॥४२॥
द्रब्य बहुत भेंट कौं मगायो । नवल देषि के हाथ न लाया ॥४३॥
यह तौ काज तुम्हारे आवे । हमकौ मदन गुपाल ही भावे ॥४४॥
परमेश्वर सौंकाज हमारौ । कहा लौ कीजै द्रव्य तुम्हारौ ॥४५॥
उदर समान प्रभु पहुचावे । कारी कामरि देह सुहावे ॥४६॥
साह कहा यह चित मति धरौ । कछू अंगीकृत यहां कौ करौं ॥४७॥
स्याम कामरी साह मगाई । नवलही अपने हाथ उढ़ाई ॥४८॥
बिदा भए बृदावन आए । इतह बिधि दूसर सब छुड़वाए ॥४९॥
साधु मिले साछू ह्वै जाई । साधु मिले सब साध पुजाई ॥५०॥
साधु मिले परमारथ होई । साधु न समझे स्वारथ कोई ॥५१॥
साधु सदा बोले मधुबानी। साधुनि की गति साधूनि जानी ॥५२॥
दोहा : परदुष दुष परसुषी सुषी भगवत हरिजन सोई।
श्री राधावल्लभ तिनहि कौ सदा सहायक होई ॥५३॥

---

1. Akbar.
2. Gentleman Troopers.
3. Blanket of Shawl.

Index